There Came a Day *is neither fiction nor TV drama. This is real life in the raw. Each chapter is filled with the unimaginable: a monstrous paedophile, a child murdered, a family devastated. Yet the darkness is pushed back by the unexpected light emanating from the broken heart of a remarkable mother – a light put there by a loving Saviour. Beautifully written, Patricia Cardy holds nothing back in this page-turner. She gives us her heart to hold for a while, and we can feel it beating... beating with love for her murdered child and remaining family, but also beating with an unshakeable trust in the Saviour she has found faithful in the worst of days. Thank you for the privilege Patricia.*

Catherine Campbell, author of *Broken Works Best*, and *Journey with Me*

Patricia Cardy has written a moving account of her tragedy. Anyone who has been the victim of extraordinary suffering can find encouragement by reading this. The kind of suffering Patricia describes does not come to most people, but it did to her. If you have been faced with severe suffering, or know someone who has, do read this book and pass it on.

R.T. Kendall, former pastor of Westminster Chapel, London, and author of over 50 books

THERE
CAME
A DAY

THERE CAME A DAY

A CHILD'S MURDER, A MOTHER'S SURVIVAL

PATRICIA L. CARDY

Copyright © 2021 by Patricia L. Cardy

First published in Great Britain in 2021

British Library Cataloguing in Publication Data
A record for this book is available from the British Library

ISBN: 978-1-913278-44-1

Designed and typeset by Pete Barnsley (CreativeHoot.com)

Printed in Denmark by Nørhaven

10Publishing, a division of 10ofthose.com
Unit C, Tomlinson Road, Leyland, PR25 2DY, England

Email: info@10ofthose.com
Website: www.10ofthose.com

1 3 5 7 10 8 6 4 2

CONTENTS

Jennifer, school photo, 1981

INTRODUCTION

Wakefield High Security Prison holds 700 of the most violent and depraved men in Britain. These are men whom society would choose to forget. Their crimes have conferred upon the jail the title of Monster Mansion. I was to discover that this prison housed a man I had long feared to meet. Years had passed without knowing his name, without having to look on his face, and without having to confront his depravity.

Robert Black had evaded capture while continuing to terrorise and kill little girls for over a decade. For this man there came a day. Once arrested, he spent the remainder of his life in prison, latterly in Northern Ireland, where the Public Prosecution Service had charged and the jury unanimously convicted him of the paedophile abduction, sexual abuse and murder of our nine-year-old daughter, Jennifer. While being held in Maghaberry High Security Prison during the trial, he applied for a permanent transfer from Wakefield.

We have all had our dark days. I have written this book hoping you will accompany me through dark days of my own. We will never understand why some things happen, not on this side of eternity anyway. Certainly, God knows. And this same God, if we trust Him, can see us through all of our days, however dark they may prove to be.

Many have written about Robert Black. I have no wish to highlight the depth of his evil. My purpose is to bring a surprising and welcome clarity that whatever your days do bring forth, we are never at their mercy.

We live in a world fraught with worry and depression of all kinds. A world which, for many, is governed by fear and undergirded with an abject helplessness. But there are answers.

We do not choose our days, we cannot change our days, nor can we relive any of them. Probably we would if we could. Throughout our days, whatever they will be, let us determine that we too will learn to know and trust God to see us through.

Come with me. I can bring you through dark tunnels, dark days, and show you this, our glorious Engineer. Maybe you will trust Him too.

1

THE DAYS WHEN WE DIE

The Bible states, "it is appointed for men to die once" (Hebrews 9:27).

I take issue with that.

It was true for Jennifer, at nine years of age. On that score I agree. Death is a one-time thing. For our daughter, there came a day. Death, however, can take more lives. There are those, still alive, who also die. For Andrew and I, we both died that same death at the same hands of the same murderer. Jennifer's brothers, Mark and Philip, learned the ongoing reality of death. That day, Jennifer also left a little sister, Victoria, a baby of eight months old, the last person she spoke to before leaving home as she reluctantly cushioned her again into my arms – though not without her well-practised giggly hug. Robert Black not only robbed Victoria of a loving sister, but he robbed her of a beautiful and irreplaceable relationship. And so, within our days, we die our deaths; few do not.

Robert Black had plunged many defenceless children to early deaths before having to await his own appointment with death in a prison hospital. He was sixty-nine and due to serve another twenty years of four life imprisonments without parole. For our family it was an unexpected phone call on the 12th January 2016: Black had just died in prison of natural causes. Whether we like it or not, God makes His own agenda.

As I slowly replaced the phone, my mind had taken on an inability to function and my mouth struggled for words as I conveyed the news to Andrew. He took it in similar silent fashion. But sense took its hold, as my heart immediately ached for a family in England whom I knew would be suffering more painful consequences of this man's death.

The name Tate brings sympathy from the people of the UK. In August 1978, thirteen-year-old Genette Tate was abducted. Shocked viewers watched television images of an overturned bicycle left abandoned, and newspapers strewn across a country lane in Aylesbeare, Devon. Little did we then know that three years later we were to face the same trauma. While there are striking similarities in the two disappearances, one major difference remains: Genette's body has never been recovered. Her case has become the longest unsolved child disappearance in British history.

Over three decades after Genette's death, the Tate family had begun to live with a new hope. In Robert Black's trial and conviction in 2011 at Belfast and Armagh Crown Court, Prima Facie evidence would give rise to the allowance of similar submissions in any subsequent trials of Black. The alleged murderer was about to face trial, conviction and further imprisonment. The police were very soon to charge Robert Black with the murder of Genette Tate.

After decades of examination, and only weeks away from the police completing their investigation, Black died. The Tate family were barely able to carry on. Knowing this, I felt their despair.

A television news report the following day recorded Genette's father's distress. He spoke of his hope that a letter might have been left in Black's cell, confessing to Genette's murder. He also revealed that he had attempted to visit Black in prison. He ended the interview by saying, "Where do we go now?"

The media interviewed us on national and local news. While many would be expecting us to say how glad we were to hear of his death, even expecting us to say how he could rot in hell, as Christians, we had neither joy nor satisfaction. Eternal hell has no return. There can be no gladness in that.

Five years earlier, Andrew had given these words on behalf of us all outside court the day of the jury's unanimous guilty verdict, "We leave the court so happy that justice has been done, and Robert Black will never again be able to harm another wee girl. He will be in jail until he dies."

Truer words have been seldom spoken.

Like Genette Tate's father, I shared a deep desire to speak with Robert Black, though wondering if, given the opportunity, I would have the guts to do it. I will never know. Nevertheless, I wanted to ask him one thing, and I rehearsed the words again, "Robert, you have done little that has been good in your life. This is one good thing only you can do. You alone can and must tell grieving parents where each of their daughters' bodies lie; bodies that you disposed of. You still see their faces. You still hear their cries. You know where you have hidden them. This is one good thing only you can do – perhaps, the only good thing you will ever do."

All these years, and with every other recorded murder of other little girls since Jennifer, my heart dies another death. We know there are still many unsolved disappearances in the UK and Ireland, and further afield in Europe, which bear the hallmarks of Robert Black. The terrible blight upon such parents is one with which so very few can identify. It has caused incredible pain, and to such parents no reunion in this life will ever come. Neither can there come a day when they will know anything of the final hours of their little children.

Young teenagers, loud and laughing on their way home from school. Their noise filled one of the busiest streets in Lisburn, our local town. It was the day after Black had died. They took my attention, my face beginning to mirror their smiles. Then, suddenly I stopped smiling, for I recalled the time when Robert Black was a similar age to these boys. A twelve-year-old, younger than those before me, when he raped his first victim. At that young age he entered the addictive cycle of sexual cruelty. In that moment I saw the vulnerability of the innocence in the boys around me. I was scared for them as I watched. Childhood adolescence ought to be innocent: I hope for the most part it is.

After Black's death, the Prison Service cremated his body. Little was said. His remains were disposed of at sea. It took Andrew and me by surprise when asked to make our views known on how we would prefer to see Black's remains interred. Answering questions on a radio programme from our home, I was glad that Andrew and I had earlier discussed this. Interested in World War II history, Andrew recalled the story of the hangman, Albert Pierrepoint who executed many Nazi criminals. On one such occasion there was a shortage of coffins and he is reported to have said that "A condemned prisoner is entrusted to me after decisions have been made which I cannot alter. He is a man, she is a woman, whom the church says still merits mercy. The supreme mercy that I can extend to them is to give them and to sustain in them their dignity in dying and in death. This gentleness must remain."

After Andrew had finished his story, I added that Albert Pierrepoint accorded respect to the bodies of some of the worst war criminals in history. And this, I thought, was a principle that applied in this case. Robert Black would meet with a God more holy than us. In his lifetime, he too had an opportunity to receive the gift – the amazing gift – of forgiveness, redemption and new spiritual life from this holy God. Many may take my words in a completely wrong context, but I make no apology when I say I would be pleased to know he did. For, I remember a little nine-year-old girl, and I remember her gladness in the gift God gave to her at that tender age of seven. Has Jennifer given Robert Black a welcome smile? I think, perhaps she has. For God says, "I have no pleasure in the death of the wicked" (Ezekiel 33:11).

2

DAYS BRINGING QUESTIONS

The biscuit tins finally made an appearance. In London, horses were becoming impatient. The red, white and blue bunting, raised some weeks previously, had taken a more commanding significance. Everyone waited, and watched.

"Mummy, there's the coach!" The little girl's usual soft voice now choked with new excitement. "I see her. She's beautiful. Look, she's so beautiful."

It was Wednesday 29th July 1981. Royal Wedding Day. And Jennifer, with all of us (even Andrew) watched enthralled. The unfolding of this royal occasion, a Public Holiday, had our eyes glued to the television set. Prince Charles, the heir to the throne, would marry Lady Diana Spencer in St Paul's Cathedral.

This summer we had decided not to have a holiday away but to make needful improvements to our newly-built house. This had become a well-detailed work in action. During Andrew's two weeks at home, he managed to convert an empty room into a fully-fitted youth emporium. Our eldest son Mark, recently a teenager, soon took proud ownership of the completed bedroom. A lot was happening at Number 32. That same day of the royal wedding, a little nine-year-old girl was not only ecstatic about the Prince and Princess of Wales, but had just learnt she could have her own new bicycle. I often wonder who had the beamiest smile that day – the new Princess of Wales, or the new cyclist, Jennifer Cardy.

Jennifer's friends often cycled to our house and while she longed to join them, she had outgrown her bicycle. It was a short walk that afternoon for Andrew and Jennifer to the local bicycle shop, a well-known and well-frequented one in Ulster. We loved our new house, having lived in rented accommodation for ten years, and had got to know our new neighbours, some of whom had small farms. The walk down was easy enough, the return journey an uphill exercise. Philip, aged six, and his friend John, our neighbours' son, kept vigil at our gate to be the first to see them return, Jennifer glowingly pushing the new red bicycle up the hill. We all knew red was her favourite colour.

We took photos in memory of the occasion. Victoria, our new seven-month-old, excitedly included. Jennifer with her new red bicycle wearing the same clothes and shoes which she wore on the dark day two weeks later.

Two years earlier while in hospital for a one-off surgical procedure, my surgeon recommended I undertake a sterilisation operation. I was twenty-seven years old and had recently become a diabetic. He awaited my decision while Andrew and I thought about it. We already had three healthy children. Philip, our youngest, was a delightful four-year-old, and, at that stage, although not planning for any more, we had certainly not ruled it out. Why should I not have more children? I knew it was in God's hands and sought an answer from the Lord. For several weeks we had none. His answer, as every believer knows, is the only wise one. Driving along the road several weeks later, I was almost transfixed on autopilot when God gave me His answer. "Have the operation. Have it now."

I can still pinpoint the place on that road where He spoke to me and with this came an immediate confidence. No reasons given. I knew I needed none.

Why this should be, I could not understand. I loved the delightful family that we had. Mark was in his first year in secondary school, Jennifer, in her third year at primary school, and Philip, still at home enjoying the country high life with noisy mud-bespattered tractors, combine harvesters, and all kinds of raucous farm machinery. Life was good. The surgeon carried out the procedure a few weeks later, and both he and my GP were satisfied with the result. While I was also satisfied, I did wonder what this all meant nearly nine months later, when nausea seemed to make a daily occurrence.

"Andrew, I think I'm pregnant. I know I must be pregnant."

A well-known and well-used Ulsterism will always make us feel uncomfortable, "Pat, catch yourself on! You couldn't be!"

It certainly makes the hearer aware that no one is taking them very seriously!

Almost everyone said the same thing. But I didn't blame them. It was the typical reaction.

I was fast becoming familiar with daily morning sickness. Why did no one believe me? A few more weeks passed while my poor husband did his best to laugh. In those days there were no personal pregnancy testing kits. Telling no one, I decided to see the doctor. Those words, "Pat, you could not be pregnant," were becoming wearying, though understandable. My doctor would know to believe me.

"Well, Mrs Cardy," said my doctor with a wry smile, as he set before me his surgical notes, using these to show how well pleased he was, not only with the reports of the done-deal operation, but in similar fashion how he could professionally, though nicely, challenge my personal diagnosis. "There is a bug going around at present. Doubtless, you should see a recovery over the next few days."

I ably identified with Chicken Licken when she declared that the sky was falling down!

Doctor Hyndman, when I saw him again a short while later, this time heeded my earnestness taking the given test to our local hospital himself. Expectantly awaiting a negative result, he quickly asked for a re-analysis when he found out the initial result. I saw him the next day and we looked at each other in stunned silence. I was definitely pregnant.

Victoria, our beautiful little "bug", was born the week before Christmas 1980. Due to my diabetes, I had been in hospital for six weeks before her birth, and allowed home at weekends. Throughout the entire pregnancy both baby and I were extremely well looked after. I did get to know lots of the antenatal medical staff, plus all the trainee doctors who constantly besieged my bedside viewing the tell-tale scars of sterilisation. Good-humoured witticisms quickly followed. It was a happy time, and I remember that as we laughed we quickly noticed that the baby who had visited my womb seemingly laughed with us, hiccuping on all such occasions – which made us laugh even more, especially me!

So, I had my questions. I prayed about my questions. I knew so well that I could easily have had this child in the normal way. What was God doing? Before having my last prenatal scan in hospital, I hardened myself to accept the fact that this child could perhaps be born with problems. I reckoned He would want me to know that, if anything were amiss with this child, I would know that in His hands He had permitted it. Maybe this was the reason, and I quietly steeled myself to be ready. But Victoria was born healthy and perfect, growing up to be her own girl, her own woman, with her own mark on life. Let's leave all our whys to the One who knows all the answers. We are never expected to be spiritual masterminds. Our days are ever in His hands, and for all the right reasons. Some months later, Scripture confirmed this to me with a loving and unforgettable reminder: "Adam knew his wife again, and she bore a son and named him Seth, 'For God has appointed another seed for me instead of Abel, whom Cain killed'" (Genesis 4:25).

3

AN IMPOSSIBLE DAY

The royal couple, still on honeymoon, knew nothing of the order of events in Ballinderry. I had just made lunch, sliding wobbly poached eggs onto several slices of hot buttered toast. Philip was getting ready to go with his friend to the swimming pool in Antrim. Mark soon left to cycle to his friend's house nearby.

We so loved this new family, even to the purchase of an estate car that could hold all the needful accoutrements for our outings together. They were proud times when we parked the car and unloaded four children, with pram, picnics, coats (always coats in Ulster) and Wellington boots. Victoria was growing quickly, ably helped by her brothers and sister who grabbed every opportunity to initiate specialised mobility classes. These consisted of Jennifer's never-failing expertise, patience and rib-cracking humour, in giving crawling lessons, together with her apprentice teacher Philip.

One of the last things Jennifer asked me to do for her that day was to make sure her red watch, received as her ninth birthday present, was set to the correct time. My remembering the time became a crucial matter in what was later to happen. I checked it showed 1.40 p.m., also checking she had secured it well on her wrist.

It was school holidays and Jennifer was looking forward to her first trip to the "Good News Club" camp – gathering with friends in a nearby home, learning songs, answering quizzes and hearing wonderful Bible stories. Having just reached that important qualifying age of nine, Jennifer and her friends excitedly awaited their first ever camp. The pretty harbour town of Kilkeel in the Mountains of Mourne was the chosen setting. It was Wednesday 12th August, and the next day we had planned to go to a church friend's house to pick out a new dress. She would leave on Saturday. This was to be her last day out on her red bicycle.

Hadn't she proved herself more than capable on our quiet country road when I had walked with her to see how well she handled the bicycle? Somehow, there was a strange heaviness with me as she left that day to visit her friend, Louise. The last sighting I would ever have of our little girl was the imprint of her fair hair sweeping around her face as she closed the half-glazed door behind her: this happy child who had continually delighted and lifted each of our lives.

The day was warm, slightly humid. Victoria sat with me on the patio of our back garden. She was in her pram. I was in my garden seat. I remember wishing it would rain. If it did, Jennifer might hurry back, but it didn't rain, and she didn't hurry back.

It was strange not to see her back at the usual time, 4.20 p.m. This was *Jackanory* time. She always enjoyed hearing these stories on television and it was already 5 p.m. Not only was it strange, but it was now becoming worrying.

"Where's Jennifer?" asked Andrew when he arrived home from work at 5.30 p.m.

He could see from my face that I was worried. We had no phone, and I could not drive my car that day because it had a puncture. Still, Andrew could not see any reason for worry. She might have stayed longer at Louise's. However, I knew she would not do that. Jennifer was always punctual, always wanting to be home on time. Indeed, she had never been late. Yes, I was worried.

We had both been aware of a deep oppression during those last few weeks and months. I still wonder about that. While we were so happy, so thrilled at the goodness of God in what was this inexplicable gift of our new daughter, we each found ourselves darkly mindful of such foreboding. Andrew had spoken to me of the fact that he had sensed an urgency to increase life insurance. I thought I was the only one who wrestled with these emotions. In Ulster, at the time of the late-seventies and early-eighties, the "Troubles" were in full force. Many, too many, innocent people were on the receiving end of

IRA threats upon their lives. Some were even killed. In an unnerving way, we assumed we had a reason for our fears.

Andrew quickly repaired my punctured wheel and I lost no time in searching for her. Reaching Louise's house, I rang the doorbell; trying to shake off the cold fear that had now given me weak, unsteady legs. Some camouflaged sanity told me I was being stupid. The answer from Louise and her Mum that Jennifer had not arrived that day shunted me to some desperate unreality. Not wanting to cause worry at this stage, I casually tried to remark that Jennifer must have gone to another friend's house in the area. I would soon find her, I told them. From their grey faces I knew I was not successful.

Driving quickly, the only words with which I could identify as I reached each of her other friends' homes were, "No, Jennifer's not here."

At each door, with many I knew so well, I heard my voice becoming thinner, my lungs forgetting their duty to breathe. No one had seen her. I still refused to panic.

"Please Lord wake me up. Please get me out of this nightmare!"

Making my way home, with an alien feeling of not belonging, I expected to see Jennifer running to the car as I turned into our drive. I so longed to see her face, to hear her cheery laugh again. Jennifer had not arrived, I could not awaken.

Immediately on hearing of my unsuccessful attempts, Andrew reversed his own car to do a wider search with me, Philip and Victoria. This time we went to as many places as we could think of, stopping, calling her name, but all to no avail. Andrew then took our neighbour and good friend Wesley with him on a broader search as I stayed with the children. Wesley and his wife, Alma, loved Jennifer, having a family of the same age, and I knew their pain on hearing of her disappearance. Bertie, another neighbour, joined them in the search. (Bertie soon became known as the last person who had seen her passing that day. He had watched her cycle until she was out of sight. As an elderly man, I don't think he ever recovered from this.)

While Philip played, my heart lifted as I watched him. I envied his innocence as he scampered about, this happy little six-year-old boy unaware that this family was now being borne into untold heartbreak. Alone, I sat under a garden tree, embracing Victoria. It was here Jennifer had sat those happy two weeks earlier with Victoria on her own lap and Philip beside them, that I had taken such a happy photograph of the three of them together. Now in the silence Victoria and I sat alone. I prayed, but I was lost for words to pray. Thoughts, fears and dreads could not be verbalised. To put these emotions into any form of words was to establish a fearsome, yet awesome reality that could not be happening. Only God knows what and how I prayed. He hears our cry, He knows our hearts, and when we have no words, He still understands.

Andrew's search with Wesley and Bertie was intensive but fruitless. They informed the local part-time police station which was about to close for the night. The sergeant was not over-anxious, but when they returned a short time later with still no sighting of her, he phoned for support from the main police station in Lisburn just over ten miles away.

Police alerted all units and the armed troops who were stationed in the area. As radio and television news began to reach the public, the numbers multiplied to include the immediate setting up of search parties. On all our roads traffic was composed of military armed cars, police cars and traffic checkpoints. Early light would bring search dogs through all our roads, lanes, farms, fields and outbuildings; and the morning could not come quickly enough.

Our house sheltered a very frightened family, now incorporating overhead army helicopters. This was hardly a rare occurrence in this part of Ulster, we had become quite used to helicopters frequently patrolling nearby areas around Lough Neagh, but the noise of these military machines now droned loudly above us. Like Dorothy and Toto, something surreal had beamed us up and hurled us back down to a cruel hinterland. But this was no work of fiction, and here in Ulster we had no yellow brick road.

Midnight! There had been no accident. Police brought us the report that neighbours had discovered her bicycle. They had driven down our road with a pick-up truck equipped with a spotlight and sighted it, glistening in the darkened undergrowth. It was then that we imagined the sinister reason as to why the bicycle was hidden in thick hedging and trees, its stand still in park position. Jennifer had been abducted! Family, friends, and our church elders who were with us, gave us time to be alone.

In stunned silence we clung to each other. It was then, while we silently embraced, with only a small morsel of strength between us, that I became aware of a rod of steel beginning from my feet and working up my body, taking the place of my crumbling spine.

I said to Andrew, "It's okay. We'll get her back. We'll find her."

Later Andrew would tell me, "That night when I held you, I felt strength within you that I knew I did not have."

Andrew, although then not trusting in Christ, would also come to know God's amazing undertaking in all that was to take place. Our family and friends left. Our last words to them were, "Tomorrow, we'll find her tomorrow!"

4

DARK DAYS

It proved a tortuous night. The morning brought little relief.

During those harrowing days, all of our family, friends and neighbours became our constant source of help and encouragement. Northern Ireland, while knowing too much of bombing, guns and murder, was ignorant of the concept of paedophilia. Television, radio and newspapers, while constantly covering the search and investigation each day, were never invasive but did bring the whole country, and the whole of the UK, together in an unforeseen way, as both sides of our broken community, and our broken country, united in the search for Jennifer.

We watched the news coverage, glad that her photograph was paramount on both local and national television. The happy face of this little nine-year-old schoolgirl was on every lamppost, every building and along every country road. Someone, somewhere, must have seen her. As we saw her familiar picture each day, we were now caught in a fabricated parallel universe; some cruel virtual reality.

"Jennifer is here, this is where she lives! She will run in at any minute! I can hear her laugh."

The truth that this might never happen again crushed us.

The mail, delivered in sackfuls to us each day, was humbling. We felt indebted to our Irish natives, and to all those much further afield, who took us into their hearts, engaged with us in prayer, and thoughtfully communicated their love in so many ways. No one will ever appreciate what it meant to have that support. We still meet many who, after more than thirty years, have never forgotten Jennifer. After some days, the police asked to take all the letters in order to examine them for clues. I felt the guilt of not being able to reply, but we read each letter and valued each one.

With our two boys, we found ourselves in the horror of ever-decreasing circles, leading faster to ever-deepening darkness. How do you try to share with your children what has happened, or what may have happened, to their sister? We were unable to tell them. We couldn't even tell Mark, who would have understood, what the police were doing, especially the underwater divers searching the depths of Lough Neagh a mile from our house.

As I look back on those days, I often wish I could go back to that time with a lot more wisdom to help

Mark and Philip, but none of us knew what another day would bring. We lived our lives, not with the comfort of hindsight, but on the run, thinking, saying and doing that which seemed most reasonable. I don't think we always got it right. At their age, life ought never to storm such shock.

Victoria became our lifeline, bringing us some meagre semblance of normality. She still needed our constant attention, and although this would not, nor could not, begin to distract any of us from the horror we had entered, caring for her provided each of us a reprieve.

The search parties were becoming wider and more intensive. For ourselves, we were now on the fine line of exhaustion. How good people can be. Many supplied us with meals, few were surprised by our lack of either need or appetite. Our two quietly tearful, question–asking boys welcomed the help given from family, friends and neighbours. While every morning came with a new hope that we would find Jennifer, each day ended with the same cutting anguish.

Mark slept in his newly converted bedroom on the ground floor, and he was able to have friends stay with him at any time. Thirteen was too young to be a man, but also too old to be a child. We watched him become quiet, and while we understood, we couldn't bring him the relief he needed. Philip posed another painful problem, trying to live life as only a six-year-old could. He was incredibly active, and we were glad to see him playing, but nothing should be stealing his innocent joy

25

of life. I was desperate to know how I could bring calm to these anxious boys.

Those early days were becoming harder at Philip's bedtime. We felt the loneliness as we walked in pain hand-in-hand past Jennifer's empty bed. Unknown to each other, I knew we both heard her laughter, remembering how her teddy and doll-covered bed would be quickly rearranged to accommodate her own giggly company. These familiar guests still lay in their lonely positions, placed in descending order of loving importance. We knew their names.

"She will be back with us soon. Of course she will!" I told Philip.

One thing did help; every evening when the search parties came to a halt, as many as could gathered in our home. William Beattie, a minister friend of Andrew, encouraged us to gather for prayer. This little epilogue service, as it became, was invaluable to everyone and I was glad to see how much Andrew appreciated it. For William, this could not have been easy. How can a young child vanish? Every tortured evening William shared God's Word of hope from the Bible, our only truth, and I could see that all who were with us took fresh breath.

On the ground floor of our house, we had incorporated quite a spacious bathroom. This became my bolthole. All that had been familiar had gone. Here I shut the door, turned the key; and here I found Jesus when each cruel day followed another cruel day. Somehow I learned to brush away new tears, finding new strength that was now finding me. The two of us were alone as I rolled on Him all my quiet screams. God has big shoulders.

When I had known nothing of Him, Jesus had first met with me. "Behold, I stand at the door and knock. If anyone hears My voice and opens the door, I will come in to him" (Revelation 3:20).

The little latch gate was steely cold as I pressed it in the darkness of that frosty October night twelve years before. Hurriedly trying to leave, the slam of car doors beckoned me to the easy familiarity I craved. I could soon be home, back contentedly to Andrew, with no rock-the-boat experience. I saw no angel, like Mary, and no blinding vision, like Paul, but I did hear, with His loving intonation, a decision, a commitment being called from me. I had to turn back.

Jesus had told it like it is. The gospel is a glorious one. It also demands a response. I was aware of my own littleness, my own dangerous unworthiness, and the naked fact that I had been found out. At least in the Garden of Eden they found fig leaves and a tree, I had neither. But God engages His truth with us in such a way that we see the enveloping of amazing love, and as I recognised this, I was conscious that this Jesus was a saving Jesus. He had died for me long ago on a cross. He had already given Himself to torture and to death, becoming my punishment and my sacrifice for all the wrong that I had done. He loved me. Jesus really loved me.

Making my way back, I pressed through the crowds of chatting people I had so quickly tried to escape from. Something had happened. I wanted forgiveness, and I wanted the peace I had needed for so long, but now I wanted Him. I wanted Jesus. I longed for what He would give me, but so much more I wanted Him. The Word so personally given from Him to me was this, "I will come in to him and dine with him, and he with Me" (Revelation 3:20).

He has ever honoured His commitment to meet with me through thick and thin, He has taken me through each of my days, sharing with me all that He is, with all that He has, with all that I have not. Jesus' personal promise that night was to make me able for each new day, no matter what that day would bring. I had so longed for Andrew to know this too, yet I was to see God giving him deepening peace and strength, fitting him also for each horrid new day.

Sense and sanity can sometimes forsake us. But God does not. On our wedding day, the pastor who married us presented a book to us entitled *Daily Light*. This devotional book held my feet to the ground. Whatever our days may bring, we need to be assured that God knows us and loves us so intimately that He can give us exactly what we need, how we need it, and when we need it.

I'd always loved the character of Jacob in the Old Testament. I identified with the fact that he was a man who did not always get it right! So Jesus, in His Word, lovingly gave me these words: "Happy is he who has the

God of Jacob for his help" (Psalm 146:5); "May the name of the God of Jacob defend you" (Psalm 20:1).

It was simple. The same God was now encouraging me. In that time I learnt to rest upon the God who proves Himself able. And, like Jacob, when there comes a day, we too shall find ourselves able for it.

5

DAYS WITH
NO NIGHT RELIEF

My sister Anne was asleep on the settee in our living room. In the early hours of the morning, wrecked with pain, I had come downstairs and, without switching on the lights, I stood in dark silence in front of the kitchen window and looked at the tree-lined horizon. Centred at the back of our garden our familiar oak tree held my gaze. Within minutes this imposing tree boasted a silent arrogance that frightened me, taunting the nothingness I was made of. There it stood, belittling my miserable awareness of a world that was too big for me. But it happened that the more I looked, even in such despair, the more I knew I had a God out there who was big. I had a God who was bigger than the amazing world He had created. I whispered the only words I was able to form, "Where is she? Where is Jennifer?"

I knew that He heard me. I knew He knew my pain. He knew exactly where she was. I waited for Him ... and I waited. Had He ever abandoned me? Had He ever ignored me? If nothing else, I waited for that fatherly warmth of everlasting arms that I had known so many times. Perhaps that would do. But I felt nothing.

The darkness in my kitchen and garden pressed in. A shuddering aloneness and a strange emptiness that I had never known before became real. The God whom I boasted of, whom I loved, the God I knew, felt distant. I quietly cried for His presence, knowing that I needed it more than I had ever done before. Turning again from the window, I admitted defeat. Then I stopped. Something rose up within me, made me turn back, made me address that same darkness and made me regale heaven with the one thing I knew to be true.

"God in heaven, You are my Father. I know You are with me. I know that You know. You know where Jennifer is. I know You hear me, and I know You love me. You are my God."

I poured out simple words with what I can only describe as unfeeling gut faith. I knew I had to. If I could not hear from heaven, heaven would hear from me. I returned to my bed, silent and distraught, and tried to hold on to some form of sleepless sanity.

That next evening our little epilogue service had finished. We had commended to the Lord all that had been done, and trustfully prayed for the new day. New day? Could we face another new day? Spending time with those who had remained that night, I soon excused myself to go to bed, holding tightly to two sleeping tablets that my doctor had earlier given to me. About to take them with the glass of water I was holding, I sat alone on the side of our bed, the two little tablets in my hand like sweaty captives. I began to think of the next night, and the further nights beyond. Weeks and months that I could foresee rendered their crushing hold. How long would I need to rely on tablets? How long until we would find her? Perhaps we may never find Jennifer. My life mirrored my despairing pain; but new words were holding me; soft surprising words. I recognised the Voice, "It is vain for you to rise up early, to sit up late, to eat the bread of sorrows; for so He gives His beloved sleep" (Psalm 127:2).

My heart was melting. I still do not know how those words became my own. My Bible remained unopened, my little *Daily Light* still confined to the bathroom. Right now, God Himself was again beside me, promising to give me sleep, and freeing me from the tablets in my hand.

I remembered that previous empty night, which I longed to forget. As I now sat here alone, that love of which I had felt so bereft, that love suddenly locked itself around and within me. The presence of my Father God became so real. Knowing Him now so close, I was glad that I hadn't thrown in the towel, glad I had held to the truth that I knew, and glad that I had spoken my own words to heaven. This is the walk of faith and I would learn this in the future many times and in many ways. As

Proverbs 3:5 reminds us, faith is acting as if the Word of God is true, even if it doesn't feel like it.

His touching nearness allowed new tears to fall. I placed the two tablets on my bedside table and shared my worship and love to the One who would never let me go. This amazing One had committed Himself to be with me through everything. As I thought of the truth of being His beloved, sleep did its business and I slept. Later I would learn how all our immediate family also slept. I never did keep those tablets.

"Christ alone, Cornerstone,
Weak made strong in the Saviour's Love.
Through the storm, He is Lord. Lord of all."[1]

We often sing this song in church. It still holds me in its beautiful truth.

The fifth day, Monday, and one television reporter interviewed Andrew asking him if he thought Jennifer was still alive.

Grief etched on his face, he replied, "The mornings are always the worst time for us, not knowing what that day may bring, but as the day goes on with her still unfound, our hope rises that she must be still alive. We appeal to anyone who has Jennifer, 'Let her go, let her wander, someone will find her. Let her go.'"

---

[1] Extract taken from the song *Blessed Be Your Name* by Beth and Matt Redman. Copyright © 2012 Hillsong Music Publishing (APRA) (adm. in the US and Canada at CapitolCMGPublishing.com) All rights reserved.

Days arrive, with their gall to follow another, as though it does not matter, as though they hold a right to do so. The next day called itself Tuesday, and somehow it had become the sixth day since we had last seen her, and for Andrew his seventh. The word "disappearance" was affecting our lives with an eerie normality. Meanwhile police brought us the needful updates, and loving, neighbouring faces brought us broad shoulders.

Since we first met as young teenagers Andrew and I were similarly positive-minded, always looking for the best within every situation, and able to act accordingly. We had now reached where we could go no further. Six days had jackknifed our home from comforting reality to bludgeoning horror.

It was early that bleak Tuesday morning that I faced the horror of another day. I came again, alone, to pray. Within each of us, the expectation that we would never see Jennifer again was taking its toll. My prayer that Tuesday morning was not the same as before – of the longing and beseeching upon God for her discovery – I was coming to know that the Kingdom of God is powerful.

As I came to Him that early morning, I said it as it was, to the God who knows and is able to answer our deepest need, "We cannot go on! Today. Let her be found today!"

As I said those words, head clasped in tear-filled hands, somehow, somehow, I knew the matter was resolved. Something had changed. God had given me such a strong yet gentle peace on what I had just laid upon Him. So much so that His sovereignty, His supreme power, impacted my fragile being with new assurance. Suddenly my feet were stronger; like a child jumping and throwing out their arms to the father they love, knowing and trusting he will safely catch them.

The day was grey; the same nothing happening. While civil, military and police forces, with search dogs and helicopters, spared neither time nor effort to widen their search, my brother-in-law, Maurice, convinced Andrew to come with him to the search headquarters. Andrew had stayed at home with us during those days. We needed to be together. Mark and Philip especially needed their Dad. It meant that, as a family, we could hear of any new developments as they arose. Andrew was good at dealing with the media and the increasingly present television, radio and newspaper reporters.

Expecting to meet the same day with the same anxiety, Andrew and Maurice reached the local police control centre two miles away in Aghalee. After barely two minutes, something happened. They both watched as telephones rang and rattled, and a flustered scene emerged. Police then asked them to leave. A car arrived at our home a short while later. Andrew was told by our liaison officer that a little girl's body had just surfaced and been sighted in a dam thirteen miles away on the side of a busy dual-carriageway. Police, I know, have a hard enough job to do, but for any to have to give a parent this news was gutting. Only God could have answered my prayer that day, and directed such events.

My heart will ever go out to the two young anglers who found her. Hadn't they only gone for a day's fishing? Andrew was to later thank them at the inquest.

Andrew's face, his demeanour, not only showed a new depth of despair, but I watched how he ran to bring me slowly to our garden seat where we were alone.

"Pat, they've found her," he said.

We had waited for six days and six nights for this moment. Now, together, we wept. Our beautiful Jennifer could not be dead. Life cannot make such mistakes. Andrew spoke to Mark and Philip. Our immediate reaction was relief in now knowing; but such pain took hold upon us all. Neither Andrew, myself, nor either of our two sons can own the remembrance of it.

Formal identification, with preparations for post-mortem, were quickly underway. I so wanted to be with Andrew as he was driven that evening with police accompaniment to the hospital morgue. He was adamant that he should do it alone, his first thoughts being that he would finally see Jennifer. He would be with her. This would be the last thing that, as her father, he could do for her. He braced himself, about to view the little body. Those standing at his side had to quickly support him.

That night in bed, we held each other.

"Pat," Andrew said softly, "we only had the lend of her!"

And I loved him for that.

6

BOOKS THAT TELL OF OUR DAYS

Books can be read and talked about. Some become more notable than others.

In the Bible book of Revelation, God tells us that He has books too. We do not know what these books contain. How many things in our lives have we already forgotten, or with some resolve kept private? For those of us trusting in Christ's death, God forgives our sins, but He does not forget all that He has brought us through. He will show nothing to be unnecessary. I think He will show impressive sovereignty upon all that He interweaves into our lives. After all, in the Old Testament, King David writes, "And in Your book they all were written, the days fashioned for me, when as yet there were none of them" (Psalm 139:16).

Jennifer entered our lives after the loss of a stillborn boy. My uppermost thought the day prior to giving birth to Jennifer was the cold fear of losing her too. Spiritually I was then becoming stronger, learning the reality of an able Saviour, and so as I prayed that day and laid on Him my fear and worry He gave me a very precious and personal promise from the Psalms, "He has blessed your children within you" (Psalm 147:13).

While I did understand the scriptural context of these words, I knew the expectancy of the birth of a healthy child. Jennifer was born on the 16th May 1972.

Mark loved her. As I watched him take time with me to hold her, he would ably chat to her, telling her his little four-year-old things. She heard his name was Mark and her name, to him, became Jemmiser.

The local Health Nurse prayed what is commonly called the Aaronic blessing upon Jennifer when she called to visit shortly after we came home, "The LORD bless you, and keep you; the LORD make His face shine upon you, and be gracious to you; the LORD lift up His countenance upon you, and give you peace" (Numbers 6:24–26). I remember the occasion, and the sense of sobriety with which the nurse held her. I also mention the gravity which it left with me, and the consequences of such a godly blessing becoming evident to all throughout her short life.

Jennifer impacted the life of our family with constant joy. Not only did she bring a sparkle to our own lives, but I was to learn from others as time passed that she had an enviable talent of lifting any heart, bringing smiles to all who were around her, and leaving an engaging warmth which belied her age to those whom she came to know. One lovely comment from the mother of one of her closest friends, a comment which will always remain with me, was that "Every time Jennifer came to our house, we were always the brighter and the better for it." There is so much I could truthfully convey, and many things which will, I suppose, never be known about her amazing young life. She is still, even in absence, a challenge and loving conviction to us all. In Luke's gospel account of Jesus' birth, after the shepherds had revealed to Mary their encounter with the angels, Luke writes that Mary "kept all these things and pondered them in her heart" (Luke 2:19). I understand that precisely.

Something significant did take place when Jennifer was only five years old. I've always kept it secret, but considering what happened to her, I feel I can now write it.

We were living in Milltown at the time. It was a usual evening on a usual day. Andrew had been working late, but I was expecting him home soon. While I waited I decided to take a quick look to check on the children, expecting them to be asleep. Philip, almost two years old, had increased this lovely family to three and I could see he was probably dreaming of further rural investigations. Sleep had also detained nine-year-old Mark, his school uniform at the ready for the next morning.

Jennifer was the last I peeped in at. I silently watched this little five-year-old sleep, but something was now taking a new hold upon me. I bent and brushed her fringe from her eyes, but became hesitant to leave. Making no noise, I did leave the room. Closing her door, as I had done with the boys, my right hand now upon the small landing balustrade, I clearly had the sense of something explicit being given to me. To my being it had neither sense nor understanding. The voice that I knew so well was compelling.

"Pray for her death!"

My body stopped, then my brain seized. This could not be real, and while I tried to think quickly with whatever scant reasoning I could muster, I felt I had no option but to drop to obedient knees. A weight upon me, a solitude of being in the presence of God commanded obedience. My hands held the cold unfeeling wood of banisters, as my knees hit the carpet. Senses made no sense. How could I word such a prayer, with no understanding of what it implied, yet feeling the magnitude of what I must now do. What I was about to say ought not to be engaged with for another seventy years, perhaps I would already be dead by then. I knew only this one thing: I could not stand again until I obeyed what God had told me to do.

I broached the words, "Lord, I now commend Jennifer to You, that You will be with her at the time and at the hour of her death."

While tightness barred me from moving, a sudden release of peace took hold of me. In some strange yet never to be forgotten way I found I needed no understanding to make human sense of what I had just prayed. It had become confirmatory: though giving me no answers. I have never forgotten those moments, nor have I ever shared them before.

I suppose we will never know all that this implies. In Scripture we see enough. How, in Egypt, did dying Jacob know to cross his hands, giving the greater Blessing to the younger son, instead of the elder? How did the archer know when to pull his bow at random, killing the disguised evil King Ahab as God had determined? It is a mystery, how God ordains what He alone has purposed, and that moment in Jennifer's life has become a solemn recollection and a gentle cushion for what took place a few years later. Such is His grace, His kindness within our lives, and for each of our days.

I was diagnosed with rheumatoid arthritis during those eight months since Victoria was born and this had brought an unexpected maturity and a loving thoughtfulness from Jennifer. Seeing what was needed, without being asked, she quickly provided a set table, cleared dishes, doing and providing needful little things for Victoria, always so quickly, and always with those twinkly smiles.

Jennifer so loved her Dad! A special father-daughter relationship was ever apparent. On the occasions when Andrew needed to work late, the floor above our living room would be loudly and perfunctorily rapped on his arrival, her shoe strategically placed beside her bed; the stairs to her room then taken two at a time. She related all daily issues to him with giggling intensity. Each Friday she loved to bring friends home from school, and on

Thursday evenings, Mark, Jennifer and Philip submitted personal lists with fine business acumen to him. He then acquired the prescribed drinks, chocolate bars, crisps and weekly comics, which were shared and sorted by all who were there. Our house was known to them for its happy laughable Fridays, from which it would soon prove very difficult for her young friends to pick up the pieces. My heart still melts when I see them.

We received the results of the post-mortem a short time after her body had been found. It showed that Jennifer had been strangled, then drowned while still alive in shallow water. Her underwear showed evidence of sexual abuse, but for a long time we were unaware of this. At the time, I took this to mean that she had not suffered in this fashion. Andrew, however, was more pragmatic.

7

DAYS WE DIE
MORE DEATHS

Ireland, romantically portrayed as the "Emerald Isle" and "the Land of Saints and Scholars" is a beautiful island. Its people have been known since the days of St Patrick for their love, their kindness and their camaraderie.

In 1921 the island was divided, and a border was established. The twenty-six counties of Southern Ireland were renamed Eire, while the six remaining counties of Ulster became known as Northern Ireland. Each country depicted either their republican independence from, or their allegiance to, the United Kingdom.

Since this time, Ulster has become renowned for violence and murderous cruelty between the two factions. Strong divisions had fostered bitter animosity for many years, and each of the local neighbourhoods knew the horror of death.

In May 1981, however, Ulster began to witness something very different. A number of IRA men imprisoned in the infamous H-Block in the Maze Prison – a prison, incidentally, not far from our home – began a hunger strike. The first hunger striker to die was a man named Bobby Sands. His funeral cortege was estimated to number more than 80,000 people. There would follow another nine hunger-strike deaths. While these ongoing funerals brought more violence to the streets and created heightened emotions, none of them, I believe, were more harrowing than the death of our little nine-year-old girl and the funeral that took place in our garden on 21st August 1981.

Mist, haze and darkness rob my memory of that day. I know the same is true for Andrew. What did we do? Who was with us? What did we say? All fog. All cloud. Throughout it all, though, some spotlights bring us moments of clarity and remembrance. The numbers of people, lots I knew, so many I did not; the tearful embraces when words could not express our grief. Our M.P., James Molyneaux, became a caring and sympathetic visitor. Reverend Ian Paisley took time to pray with us. The local priest who reminded us of Mary and Joseph's search for the twelve-year-old Jesus. "If Jennifer should never return here," he said, "she will surely be found in her Father's house above."

The morning of the funeral I had taken a great deal of care to dress Victoria, which I knew Jennifer would have liked. I have never felt so weak. I have never felt so frightened of my own weakness. I worried for Mark and Philip. I worried for Andrew. This day was becoming more unreal, more painful, than I had ever imagined.

When I could, I escaped to the quiet room with the locked door. I knew He was waiting. I sat alone on that bath ledge and heard Him speak to my heart, "Pat, go and get your Bible."

I quickly went to our bedroom. My Bible was sitting, as it always did, on my bedside table. The leather felt soft, as if it belonged in my hand, as if it had a right to do so.

I waited. He will show me what I need. Had He not been near to me as I took time to read my little *Daily Light* book? It had been all I had needed. Earlier I had already decided that I would remain indoors for the funeral. Everyone would understand. Exactly why I should do this, or want to do this, I really did not know. We had arranged to have her funeral outside in our front garden.

My marker was still in my Bible and, without knowing what else to do, I decided to read where I had last left off. "For our light affliction, which is but for a moment, is working for us a far more exceeding and eternal weight of glory" (2 Corinthians 4:17).

Light affliction. For a moment? This could never be called light affliction. Now uncertain if this was His Word for me, I read on, "while we do not look at the things which are seen, but at the things which are not seen. For the things which are seen are temporary, but the things which are not seen are eternal" (2 Corinthians 4:18).

Then I understood. Yes, I understood. The coffin I was about to see in my garden, the garden where Jennifer played, would exhibit, and manifest her death to me. This was my unvoiced fear, even to myself, but God knew it. I looked at the words before me, again amazed at how much our Father shall always be touched in His own heart with our deepest need and our hidden fears. I had His answer. Don't look at a coffin! How could I not? Of course, I would see it. This thought was wrecking me. Whoever had abused, tortured, strangled, murdered Jennifer would torture and strangle both Andrew and myself for the rest of our lives. The love Jennifer had shared with each of us for those nine beautiful years choked my every emotion. But I was being told not to focus on her coffin. I had been told to look at what I could not see, that which was new, eternal, true and forever.

"The things which are seen are temporary, but the things which are not seen are eternal."

Andrew and I stood in our front garden holding one another's hands, surrounded by the loving throng of family and friends, our eyes and our hearts connected as though, in the middle of all these people, there were only two: Andrew and me. I knew he had the same peace that was holding me. I was able to whisper to him that this was not hard; he squeezed my hand, as I did to him.

"No, it's not hard," Andrew said quietly.

God has a presence. It is a wonderful presence whereby we feel our own deep value to Him, even with our grief. There had come a day, a day I could not handle. On days like these, God can tenderly hold all our sense and sensibilities. The agony which held me was bringing death to my own heart. Gradually (or was it suddenly?) heaven opened her doors. Jennifer had not died. She would never die just as Jesus told all who trusted Him. That sting had gone. I recalled the words of Jesus, "Father, I desire that they also whom You gave Me may be with Me where I am" (John 17:24).

My last spotlighted memory, as the funeral directors were making efforts to bring the cortege under way to the cemetery, was to reach Victoria. My sister Anne had decided to remain indoors to look after her, and I had been unable to persuade her to do otherwise. I yet feel the chilling panic as I struggled to enter our house quickly, rudely trying to bypass sympathising friends.

Victoria was the last of our family to be with Jennifer, apart from myself, and I will always hear Jennifer laughing that last day at how much she was growing, jokingly passing her to me before she left. I brought her from inside the house to the side of the coffin; this little one who would never grow to know her, or to love her. We said our last farewell. It was a personal and poignant moment.

We had bought three plots, graciously offered to us from our local council at a small cemetery in the grounds of a four-hundred-year-old derelict church just over a mile from our house. It is still a lovely place to be and, in the years after the funeral, one we often took the children to see. Within this idyllic place were some of our neighbours' graves, and also those of our dear grandparents. The funeral procession was due to leave. They would walk the distance, pausing at the site of her abduction nine days before. Many lined the route. Another day had come, the next day. For different reasons this day for me, would also never be forgotten.

The day after the funeral. I was alone downstairs in the house. Victoria was sleeping upstairs. Lifting an examining eye around the now empty, quiet rooms, those insistent, though often unseen "clean me" images mirrored back at me. With mop and bucket, hoover and duster, nothing could soften my turmoil as I worked harder, and faster, not allowing myself a moment to think. That would be safe.

Andrew had left with two of our friends to go to the cemetery. Of course I assured him that I would be okay. Mark and Philip were glad to go with them though I knew it would not be easy. I had said that I needed to do some housework, and now was as good a time as any. I thought I was made of stronger stuff.

The regime continued, and I was in our bathroom, Victoria still cocooned in dreamland. Alone, struggling not to cry, I impressed myself that I was doing so well. In order not to cry, I forced myself not to think. That was hard. I cleaned the last room, replacing familiar items with cleaner and more hygienic ones. Finding I was still clutching some things in my hand, I looked to return them to their rightful places. But these items, when I saw them, no longer had any rightful places. I recognised them. They were Jennifer's. Her toothbrush, her little face cloth and Snow White soap, lovingly misshapen. Each was personal, well-used and much-loved. They were in my hand, like displaced refugees with nowhere to go.

Scalding tears were quick to fall.

Jennifer would never be back. I would never see her again. The little soap, often used, was now dried, forlorn and abandoned. I imagined again how Snow White would have danced through warm water in Jennifer's hands, and how we would have laughed together. Gasping sobs bullied my being as I stood alone. I had no defence. I hungered for my own death, expecting death to forbid any further intake of breath. Unable to bring a stop to my tears, I called out to the One whom I knew was close to me; even though I felt like He, even He, could not help me now.

"Lord, I want to die. I cannot live. I cannot go to her. You will not bring her to me. You cannot help me."

I felt emptied of hope. Like a tsunami that leaves nothing intact, tears wrecked me.

I sat on the bath ledge, wide enough to hold towels for the bath, easy to sit on when bathing the children. This quiet place, where I was never without Him, had been my refuge for ten days, but this was a God whom I knew to be above everything in my life, yet now I felt like He could do nothing.

"Lord, You know You can help me. Please, let me die ... please, let me die," I said.

My hands reached for that little *Daily Light* book which had helped me so much. As I tried to read, tears, unstoppable, blinded my eyes. I had read the daily reading for that morning so had opened it at a random page. His words that had given me life, His nearness that had embraced me, now seemed so futile, so far away. For the second time, I opened the book before me. Still unable to read, I could only relent to more tears. Nothing seemed to matter anymore. A sinking hopelessness had overwhelmed me. Why was it taking so long to die?

Something changed. Someone was beside me. I knew Him. Jesus was so close to me, I knew the soft gaze that held me. I felt His warm touch, and I knew as I cried that I was no longer alone. Jesus was with me. He was weeping with me. I do not know how I knew. I had not raised my head, sobs still gutted within me, but I knew a beautiful difference. Jesus never views our tears – He shares them. We wept together! My wrenching bitter sorrow, Jesus was sharing. He was on my left side and physically I felt the weight of an arm laid upon my right shoulder. I have no idea how long we sat together. Then I remember my tears being gently hushed, cries gently quietened, while I reached again to that still-opened book beside me. I lifted it, for the third time. The words before me held my eyes in an intimacy known only to His own. "And God will wipe away every tear from their eyes; there shall be no more death, nor sorrow, nor crying. There shall be no more pain, for the former things have passed away" (Revelation 21:4).

As the page ended, I read the last words, these same words were given to me the day before at the funeral, again so meaningful where I now sat. "[So] we do not look at the things which are seen, but at the things which are not seen" (2 Corinthians 4:18).

Did God end my life, as I felt I needed Him to? Did He obligingly take me to be with her, or did He return her to be with me, with all who loved her? The answer is no, but there was a difference, and Jesus is always the difference. He was with me. I had His nearness; I had Him. I knew His shared grief: God shall never ensconce Himself in ivory palaces. He is touched in all and by all that we will ever have to pass through. The depth of love that He felt for me and gave to me that day will yet hold me many times. His love will hold you. "In all their affliction He was afflicted, and the Angel of His Presence saved them" (Isaiah 63:9).

This is God. This love and this compassion are His reality. His heart is full. This God will show us His joy in lifting our eyes beyond every sorry mess that shackles us. I was to meet with Him on another occasion, here in the bathroom again. That time He would ask a question that I needed to be prepared to answer. One we all should.

8

SUMMERTIME, AND THE LIVIN' AIN'T EASY

The bathroom floor felt hard and cold but I didn't care. I had tried to voice a prayer for His help, but had slumped to the floor. Familiar tears soon wet my face. Before others I was becoming more adept at concealing tears, but not so with God. He took them. He will take us as we are, always. But I was here with God to do something I knew I should do, had to do, but knew I could not do. I knew Andrew could not do this either, but we needed to do it together. Choked prayers were torn from me. I could make little attempt to verbalise.

We were aware that Mark, Philip, all of us, had been instinctively eyeing Jennifer's toys in our living room. She had loved her Christmas present, a new Sindy doll's house. More specifically – it was a lavish Sindy apartment, which she enjoyed playing with, and sharing with her friends. Previously, we had talked to others of the loss of their own child. The one thing they had chosen to do was to leave all personal items untouched, in order that life could continue as though they were still with them. Andrew and I could identify with this, but were like-minded in knowing what we must do and, yet, also what we could not do.

Life would be lived for all of us, as life should be lived, with focus, with spontaneity, with reality. We had our two young boys and a baby girl. Jennifer would always be with us, never forgotten. We would carry and bear the pain of her loss, but we would have an ongoing life. We decided to live without shrines. We would as a family, and especially for Mark and Philip, however hard, live a life not only with a painful past but also with a hope-filled future.

Andrew has since said, "The murderer who destroyed our daughter will never destroy us or our family."

It was Tuesday morning. After taking Philip to school, and Mark having left for his school bus, I arrived home with Victoria, having arranged to meet with Andrew to sort through most of Jennifer's toys, in order to give them to the local children's home in Lisburn. It was something upon which we took time in deciding, knowing how Jennifer herself would not only have agreed with us, but also loved to do it. We knew her heart, her smiles knowingly etched before us. Andrew had arrived, at least his car was here. But when I entered our house, I found that he had actually left to go running, for him a good stress reliever. We knew how very difficult this would be, and had talked together the night before.

"How can we give anything away? Andrew, I can't do that!"

"Pat, I can't do it either, but I'll be here in the morning, and we'll do it together."

My head was heavy as I entered the house with Victoria, thinking on my unspoken words, "Why not decide, like our friends, to keep all secretly intact as if she had never left – as though she were still here? That way, we could keep her."

We had a hard decision to make. Of course we wanted the easy option: let's keep her with us the only way we know how. Keep everything untouched, unmoved. School had restarted. How hard this must have been for both our boys: Mark given sympathy from friends and teachers who could not know what to say to him, or what to do, and Philip starting a new primary school alone where Jennifer also should have been going. Andrew was back at work, with no heart, no focus, only that empty nothingness.

For me, life shouldered the same wreckage. Being a Christian cannot camouflage us from grief nor the pain it causes. Each morning, on returning from school, Jesus began to teach me how to walk a new path with Him. A great sadness filled each of us, nor could we lighten anyone's load. The anxiety I shouldered for our beautiful family, especially Andrew, was more than I could bear.

I deeply felt for him, as I watched him struggle, and therefore my words to God could only be, "I ask You now to take my hand, to walk me through where neither I nor my family are able to go."

Beginning in Genesis, I immediately found Him answering my prayer that Tuesday morning just when I needed Him.

It was then, as I was upon the floor, face in hands, that I heard Him speak to me. He was so near to me that it seemed the bathroom itself knew His presence. Only God could then say something so strange, so succinct, and so demanding of reply.

"Pat, do you love Me?"

The silence was heavy. The question demanded answer. The searchlight of His truth gave me no leeway to be vague. I must reply. He was waiting.

"Lord, you know that I love You. I so love You." I could only whisper.

Why was He asking me this? I felt like Peter, the disciple, when he was asked the same question so long ago. As I waited, God laid words upon my heart, words with an awesome revelation I had never known before.

"For God so loved the world that He gave His only begotten Son" (John 3:16).

Silence. At that moment, I knew something – had been shown something – incredible of God. My Father in heaven was engaging the reality of His heart that few are aware of, with a young thirty-three-year-old girl slumped on a cold bathroom floor. Not only was this love reaching, touching me, but the essence of His very being impinged itself upon me. I was deeply aware that such love was now revealing to me its own innate depth.

Love engenders a cost. Suddenly I realised I had taken this love of God without considering the immense cost which this love entailed. The love that God now revealed to me was the costliest and the most painful thing He has ever done. It is the costliest thing that has ever been done. If this was true, then the love which God was asking of me must also be with the same worth and consequence. Love, that I was now giving Him, must make its own surrender, with its own cost. "God so loved – that He gave." A long time ago Samuel Rutherford made this comment, "There are curtains to be drawn in Christ that we never saw and new foldings of love in Him."[2]

I sat in my silence, aware so much of His presence, that I was fearful to turn, lest I should see Him.

"For God so loved the world that He gave His only begotten Son, that whoever believes in Him should not perish but have everlasting life."

His love for me impassioned Him to give that which was His most precious. This love lifted me at the expense of His own Son. God had shown me an unforgettable lesson. He had a choice of either judging me, or giving His only Son as a fitting ransom for me. God gave Jesus to a dark world, to take upon Himself my punishment, to

---

[2]   Rutherford, S, *The Loveliness of Christ* (Banner of Truth, 2007)

live a righteous life for me when I could not do it. Because He loved me, love paid its costly price.

I answered the question. If I did love Him, as I had acknowledged, if I "so" loved Him, then like Himself in His giving of His own Son, my love for Him should bring a giving response. God was asking me to give Jennifer to Him freely, because I loved Him; to let her go, to free her and release her. In no longer wanting to keep her to be with me I found the truth of something precious. Love frees us. It frees us to worship, it frees us to serve, and it frees us to give. Unknowingly I was soon to find out that love frees us to forgive. That morning on that hard bathroom floor, I gave Jennifer to Him because I loved Him.

The opposite is also true, and I have learnt this many times. That which we find ourselves unwilling to do for Him, choosing to shun and step back from, is the sad result of a love that is failing.

Andrew and I found that day we were able together to do what we had to do. He took toys to the local children's home in Lisburn, gladly received, while many items of a more personal nature, we kept.

9

A DAY – PERCHANCE
TO DREAM

I awoke, knowing that what I had just dreamed was more than a dream. Yet while this dream had alarmed me, I brought none of it to the new day. What I did have when I woke, though, was a new appreciation of safety, protection and wellbeing. As my heart had stopped its screaming, my warm searching feet found their comfy slippers.

A high rock-faced cliff, of which I must reach the summit, was the centre-stage of the dream. Aware of danger, I could not allow any delay, so I looked for footholds as my cold hands grabbed the first outcrop of rock. Somehow, I began to climb. The further I climbed, the less able I was to look at anything below. The ground became more distant as I became more frightened. What was I doing there? Fear can petrify, and make us feel so alone, and while we dream, we have no safety of knowing its unreality. With a hammering heart, I climbed.

Then I heard the noises. Behind me dark menacing figures were screeching hideous high-pitched hisses, while razor teeth snapped inexorably as I scrambled away from them. These were demonic noises as their satanic mouths rasped hot air upon my bare heels with every slicing attack. They climbed like geckos and sounded like rattlesnakes.

Suddenly the terror ended. Still feeling the animosity as I neared the summit of the rock, a white glistening coach arrested my sight. I had never seen such grandeur. This coach was there for me – its two back doors open, its engine revving like a Formula 1 car on the Monaco Grand Prix.

Inside I saw beautiful people, urgently beckoning me, "Don't look back, don't look down, keep going. Come on!"

With my focus now on the coach, I easily scaled the remaining footholds, reaching the top of the cliff with relief. The hissing around me suddenly stopped, as did the razor-biting teeth. I didn't look back, but like a winning, albeit exhausted, athlete I joined the others within the safety of my coach. Their cheering applause lifted and overwhelmed me, and I was humbled by seeing such delight upon every face. My relief was with tears. The coach sped us away.

God had given me this dream, and when I woke up the next morning I knew the reason.

Days before, on Sunday morning, I had just arrived with our children at church. I found fellowshipping with those who knew and loved us emotionally hard. So often kindness directed to us when we feel at our most vulnerable can be the most unsettling, and the most touching.

In retrospect, thinking of those months after Jennifer's death, I am aware how very hard it must have been for Mark and Philip to be in church without their sister, and without their Dad. I do admire them for how each displayed their youthful resilience. We were quickly taking our leave of those in church when a friend, whose daughter Jennifer had known and been close to, stopped me with these words:

"Pat, as you entered this morning and passed my seat, I was reading Psalm 34, and had just reached verse 7, when the Lord impressed me to give this Scripture to you: 'The angel of the LORD encamps all around those who fear Him, and delivers them.' I don't know why, Pat, but I know I must give this verse to you." I will never forget her earnestness. Unwittingly I was soon to realise the gravity with which God takes any offence brought against His children.

It was the next morning. A Monday. A visitor was knocking on our front door. That could only mean one thing, someone I did not know. Any who did know us always used the back door to come in to our kitchen –

Ballinderry custom! I was alone with Victoria, and had become quite used to callers who would come to share their sympathy with us. It always encouraged us, and came when most needed.

The visitor looked like a nice woman and I soon made tea. She introduced herself as someone who had come a distance and I thanked her for that. I was very touched, until ... why was she saying such things to me? I tried to change the conversation, but to no avail. The lady was inflexible.

"Oh, Mrs Cardy, I can hear Jennifer scream. I can hear her scream for her Mummy. Can't you hear her scream, 'Mummy, Mummy!' Can't you hear her scream, Mrs Cardy?"

Her words became shrill: I felt her watching me as I moved away to lift Victoria, needing her baby nearness. I hoped she would bring a distraction, even enough to bring some new topic to the conversation, and as I held her I walked with her to the window. The woman was now sitting behind me. I could not look at her face. After some more minutes, the blistering words became too much for me. I could not divert her. Without choice, I asked her to leave. How quickly she was gone. Where had she parked her car? What car was she driving? I did not walk outside to wait politely for her to drive away. Such would be Ulster courtesy. I rested my forehead upon the cold, closed front door as I still held Victoria, a soft quietness enveloping us both, and I caught her little eyes upon me as though in sympathy. I wanted to cry, and I shuddered uncontrollably.

Then, there was the afternoon. I would definitely pick up in the afternoon! Another visitor did call, and I did not know this lady either. She was local, and I liked her immediately. This lovely woman cheered me as I heard from her how Jennifer had befriended and helped her little boy when he had just started school. How touched I was to hear of the thoughtful, surprising little things Jennifer had done, though feeling an unhappiness that I should never hear her tell me these things herself. My guest was quickly growing uneasy however, and as I tried to make her feel more welcomed, I was seeing that this too was a lady on a mission.

Some matter had upset her, and, with persistence on my part, she told me what she knew. With no idea what I was about to hear, I steeled myself to be ready for the uncomfortable. She had heard a conversation the previous day which had left her in deep dismay. This would have been the same time as I had heard the words conveyed to me by my friend in church. I was moved with deep concern. A cruel fact emerged. People whom we knew were beginning to accuse Andrew and myself of the murder of our own daughter. Supporting this ghastly indictment was the fact that Andy and Pat Cardy had been heard to laugh together.

Sometime earlier a couple had remained with us one evening. Their daughter had also been about to go for the first time to the same camp in Kilkeel as Jennifer, and both of them had been excitedly planning, counting the days until the coming Saturday. As we talked that night, just the four of us, both Andrew and I began to laugh as we heard and reminisced on the fun times the two girls had had together. It was so lovely to hear of little things we had not known; things that seemed so "Jennifer"! It was several weeks, even months, since Jennifer had been murdered, and it was so refreshing to hear things that the girls had said and done together.

For the first time we laughed. I expect it seems a strange thing, but the first thing to hit me in our kitchen was, "I laughed! I've just laughed!"

As we exchanged glances I knew Andrew felt the same. Neither he nor I had laughed or barely smiled, for what seemed a long, long time. We shall always treasure it.

It was evident our friends could never, even in the most literal sense of these words, be the instigation of any such rumours. We loved them: but only a little fire will make dry wood burn. Those who did twist these things to our defamation showed they had never known us. Such were the words I shared with this woman beside me. She felt so guilty in telling me, but I assured her she had been right to do so.

After she left, I brokenly came to Him. Through choked prayers, through painful "who, why, hows", I found only His love, care and gentle peace. This same peace I have known so many times. It is not a flittering emotion. It is a fortress, a rock that grips our fragile, shaking being.

The day persisted. That evening I received a telephone message, relayed to me through a neighbouring friend. How the sender of the message, the wife of the minister who had taken the epilogue services at our home before we found Jennifer's body, had known the urgency with which to pass me these words, I never did find out. Just like my friend at church the day before, she too was able to give the same urgency to me in the fact that this was her own reading that day. As she read, the Lord impressed her with the importance of it for me. The message was this, "not in any way [be] terrified by your adversaries" (Philippians 1:28).

That was it, nothing more. It was enough. God was my God, and He was in control, above all others. So He had committed Himself to be sovereign in my life and in the life of my family. Satan has blinded so many to the one fact that we have a good God, a real, personal God, who can hold us with His own strength in the face of any evil. Yet the insidious assumption of evil had met with His enabling in our lives before unbelieving, accusing eyes.

Hit by such knockout punches, little did I realise more was to come. That evening when Andrew visited the police station in Aghalee, the police were to tell him of the rumours that had come in against him. Now they asked Andrew to confirm that Jennifer was his own child. Letter, or letters, had been sent to the police station informing them that Jennifer had been fathered by another man and in their view Andrew Cardy had obviously murdered her himself in jealous rage. One of the immediate things that God was quick to give me in this wreckage was the verse in Matthew, which I had read many times, yet never thought of personally: "Blessed are ye, when men shall revile you, and persecute you, and shall say all manner of evil against you falsely, for my sake. Rejoice, and be exceedingly glad: for great is your reward in heaven" (Matthew 5:11–12 KJV).

Then the dream, coming a short time later: the dream that made sense of it all, and the Scripture, that the Holy Spirit confirmed it with: "Therefore we also, since we are surrounded by so great a cloud of witnesses ... let us run with endurance the race that is set before us, looking unto Jesus, the author and finisher of our faith" (Hebrews 12:1–2).

God was teaching me to keep my eyes upon the One who was able to keep me.

During the inquest some months later, the police spoke to the court, having heard all that had been said regarding us. They ably testified to our character, and that of our family, bringing derision upon any who would taint us with further lies. This they did generously without request on our part, and surprised us with their thoughtfulness. It is our delight to say nothing evil was ever again reported. The family knew the ongoing comfort of what the police had done for us. The verdict given was unlawful killing. Emotions are part of our lives. But with such emotions, we can pay a heavy price. And I was soon to find this out.

10

DAYS – DECIDING NOT TO LIKE HIM

Feelings. Emotions. God wants us to know that we cannot rely upon any to govern our lives. It is significant that God tells us five times in the Scriptures "the just shall live by faith" (Romans 1:17). I thought I had got a grip of that, that all I was required to do under this directive was to keep my faith in Jesus. That would be a part of the truth, but in no way the measure of it. Another learning curve was to follow.

I had arrived at an impasse. God's Word had become my strength, my only refuge. While that was always good, I was now wrestling with a verse that I struggled to believe was true. I had no problem in accepting these words, "The thief does not come except to steal, and to kill, and to destroy" (John 10:10).

If this was true, it appeared God was deriding, even mocking me with the further words of Jesus, "I have come that they may have life, and that they may have it more abundantly" (John 10:10).

A simple question – where was the truth in this? And where do I go from here? There would never, and could never, be the possibility of life for us, let alone what is called abundant life. Reality had imprinted its dim view upon that which I once held true. I found His words to be false. So I lost my trust, and I lost my respect. Looking at these words, nothing now could give me hope. I struggled with cutting unbelief. Then I backed off and fell out with God.

Dear Jacob – the dear man came to my rescue, again. A lovely way in which God has chosen to convey and reveal truth to us is by bringing us through the life steps of those we read of in the Word. Every testimony tells us, "What He's done for others, He'll do for you."

We will find His mark on His men. On first coming to faith, knowing little, the stories I began to read were of people just like me. These people did not get things easy. Life's tough, and it is tough for us all. As we read what they came through, the one amazing thing each of us can see is how personal God is. God's heart relates to all of His people. He strengthens their backs for loads they cannot bear, and He brings their feet to places they once could not stand.

Reading about my friend Jacob on his way home after many years in Genesis 32, I saw his fear deepening as he came closer to meeting Esau his older brother again.

He had dreaded this meeting for years since he left, and rightly so. Esau had determined to kill him.

A strange scenario developed: a scary meeting in the dark, alone with the God whom he most needed. In the dark of that fearful night, Jacob met God in a way he had never done before. I feel we all must. God will always meet with us within the darkness of our own fear. It was here that God, as a man, wrestled with Jacob, and here God asked the man his name. I have thought of this many times. God will, at some point in our lives, call us to own before Him who we are, and what we are, particularly, like Jacob, when we are and have nothing. I was aware that I had been looking at God, thinking only with my own emotions the which made sense to me. I knew better than He did. I took my own lonely place with Jacob. I felt the same as I had done the night I first gave my life to Him – I felt my nothingness, remembering the gravity of His words to me. I knew again the presence of Christ, and I tried to back off.

Then Jacob asked His Name. We need, like Jacob, to ask and find Him out when He holds us in the grip of a tight hand. Many times overlooked in this story is the following statement: "And He blessed him there" (Genesis 32:29). As I came face to face with God in my own darkness and disbelief, you will too. The word I could not bring myself to believe – abundant life – I had now, gladly, to submit to and believe just like Jacob did.

"Just as he crossed over Penuel the sun rose on him, and he limped on his hip" (Genesis 32:31). God left His mark upon him. God left His mark upon me. He had put Jacob's hip out of joint when they wrestled together, thus causing him pain for the rest of his life, in greater and lesser measure. We do become accustomed to Jacob leaning upon his staff. When in ongoing pain and disability, this man would never forget that lonely night in the hold of a mighty God. But something beautiful entered his going, "the sun rose on him"! Right then, I too knew the sun would shine upon me, and I knew the sun would always rise upon me.

"I have come that they may have life, and that they may have it more abundantly."

Jacob had become my object lesson again. I was about to throw in the towel but had just learned that if this man could walk the road where life would take him, then with the same God I could too. There would be a lifetime of more, and of less, painful days for Jacob; there would be those same painful days for me. But as upon Jacob, the sun will always rise upon each of us.

"The just shall live by faith."

The words of Stuart Hamblen's well-known song "It Is No Secret" were written on the recommendation of a friend. This friend had seen and heard of a great change in the life of Stuart. Stuart had been a drinker and brawler, and had spent many spells in jail. The friend asked him how this change had happened and was told in these words, not yet written in song:

"It is no secret what God can do,
what He's done for others He'll do for you."

The friend suggested that Stuart, a songwriter, should "turn that into a song". The friend who asked him was John Wayne.

When we hear of what God has done for others, let's believe what He can and will do for us as well. We will live, not only upon our saving faith in Christ who has done all for us, but we will live each day upon the truth, the integrity and the power of His written Word. He had shown me that whatever things may look like, or feel like, I can and I must submit to His written truth. His Word is big; it is bigger than me, it is bigger than you. If God tells us that we will have a life, and have it more abundantly, we will put our money where our mouth is, believe it, and "live by faith"!

11

HARD DAYS WITH A HAPPY GOD

Christmas, and the shops were merrily ringing it out, television advertisements made much of the man in red and decorated trees were twinkling. I thought of the year before. I had been in hospital for six weeks before Christmas, expecting the birth of Victoria, and was only home with the family at weekends. For once at Christmas, the world may never see such again, I had been organised. I had thought of, bought and wrapped everything. Well, Andrew did find himself with some to-do lists. The previous year had been so special, we were all finding however, that Christmas is only happy when life is happy. It can be the saddest of times. We all dreaded it. Andrew and I both had already decided to keep up the festivities. As a family, we needed to. I continually wondered how that could be possible. The weeks and months were raw, incredibly painful, and only seemed to become more so. I did however (in fact, we all did) try to put on that brave Ulster face.

At church, we had our usual Women's Meeting, and had gathered to sing carols. It was hard, but I congratulated myself on seeing it through. It was the closing words I could not believe when I heard them spoken.

"How can we end our service without singing this beautiful children's carol?"

I quietly choked as everyone smiled. Those sweet familiar words that we all love, "Away in a manger, no crib for a bed", were wrenched from me, with gutted and determined composure.

"Pat, just do it … make yourself do it!"

All voices melted in my hearing into some nebulous background noise, including my own, while the only voice I heard was Jennifer's, happily singing the carol which she loved. My heart wept, as my tongue and throat refused to engage. As we closed our meeting, I made an escape to the bathroom, and tried hard to keep tsunami tears at bay. No way would I allow others to feel sadness on my account. They did not need that, and I quickly left for home.

I should say here that this has been a particular issue which I know I ought to have addressed in many ways and at many times. Independent-mindedness is not always good. Unfortunately, I have become quite adept at it. Friends ought to be trusted with our hurts, with our "can't do's", and with our "don't know how to's".

Bringing Philip home from school one afternoon the dread and fear of Christmas became more unliveable. Again barely holding back tears, with little Philip in the back seat as I positioned the car to enter our driveway, I heard the Voice. The one Voice that now I knew so well as always, it was only Him, only me.

"Why can't you celebrate Christmas?"

I heard nothing more, and I knew nothing more was needed. God speaks without duplicity, never needing explanation. We know. We just know. Suddenly my heart lifted.

How could I have dreaded celebrating Christmas? How could I ever wish to have no more Christmases when God had just impacted my sad heart with the understanding that Christmas is His own joy upon our lives. This beautiful little girl was in the reality of a wonderful eternal heaven because of that first Christmas Day. The first Noel 2,000 years ago epitomised a unique angelic choir filling our sky with the message of heaven, not only for a few shepherds but for Jennifer, for you, and for me. God loves our celebration of it, and I will always be blessed in His delight to share the angels' words with me.

"Glory to God in the highest, and on earth peace, goodwill toward men!" (Luke 2:14). They sang, filling the sky with joy. Their hearts, never seen before nor after, seemed to spontaneously combust in what Jesus had at last come to do. For those who are without dear ones that they love, Christmas will be bleak. Christmas without Jennifer was bleak. In many ways it was empty for all of us. For me, in the driveway of our house, heaven was near, and heaven has ever become more real.

As on all our Christmas Days, we had Andrew's parents with his brother, Tom, and sister, Elizabeth, come round. We learned to help each other and staggered through the day. Victoria was a beautiful smile-giver, turning one year old earlier that week, and an able smile-bringer from saddened Mark and Philip. All our hearts were lifted. I loved Andrew's and his father's positivity, which encouraged each of us that sad day.

What remains with me each year on a more personal level, albeit more than thirty years later, is the driveway remembrance of His godly question. Maybe you need to take it to your heart.

"Why can't you celebrate Christmas?"

Some years had passed, none of them easy. I think, as a Christian, the most precious thing I learnt in a new way was the heart of our Father God. While I often found it hard to cope, and some days the reality of what had happened to Jennifer would cruelly hit me, I also grappled with issues that were just too much for me. One thing I relied on, and the one thing that bolstered my sinking faith, was the newly revealed truth of the Lord's Prayer.

Sometimes we have no words, and are unable to convey our own need, even to ourselves. God does not require us to be articulate. Just to say those two words, "Our Father", became so intimate, so endearingly personal and so real.

And so God helped me to understand that He was not just giving me words to say as a prayer, He was blessing me with the truth that I was His child. He cared for me, and He will always be there for me, never aloof, never condemning, and never without precious, enabling grace.

Oddly enough, Jesus never directed us to address God as "Almighty God", "Creator God" or "Holy God". While these noble titles are wonderful in their own right, God's heart is such that we each should know and approach Him in this deeper capacity that He has brought us into. And so I made this God-given prayer my own. I was learning to take it phrase by phrase, meaningfully and personally. It brought to my heart sweet revelation, and continues to do so. "For your Father knows the things you have need of before you ask Him. In this manner, therefore, pray" (Matthew 6:8–9).

In the Old Testament, Job's declaration often gives people mixed feelings. Job, after the loss of all his children, said to his friends, "The LORD gave, and the LORD has taken away; blessed be the name of the LORD" (Job 1:21).

Church friends warmly conveyed these words to us when hearing of Jennifer's body being found.

He gave Victoria. He took away Jennifer.

He had wonderfully given this gift of a child. We were also to know the sadness of losing Jennifer. We do well here to keep in mind that God has no affiliation with the evil of her taking.

There is great comfort and encouragement in these words of Job, but let us not put the emphasis on the negative. But more importantly let us do what Job did. He blessed His Name. The same good God who gives is ever the same good God who may take. There is the difference. His love never diminishes, His goodness never fades and His purpose is never thwarted. If we can trust such a God in good times, we can surely trust Him in bad. Let's put it this way – it will serve for our good, for our enabling and for His glory.

We had chosen to visit Jennifer's grave on anniversary occasions – her birthday, Christmas and the anniversary of her death, though of course there would be others. On one occasion I was visiting the grave alone, arranging flowers, and as I sat on the rock outcrop beside her grave, as I would, I felt frightened, very frightened, and very alone. Other times when I had been, this had been my little "Ebenezer", "Thus far the Lord has helped us" (1 Samuel 7:12), a time of quietly reflecting on the real goodness of a real Saviour. Memories of Jennifer brought their delight, though painful, as I watched her in my mind laughing again with her friends.

Thoughts were engulfing me, thoughts now commanding my guilt. It was now more than I could bear.

"This was all my fault," I said to myself.

I was aware that I would bear this cruel guilt for the rest of my life.

"I should never have let her go that afternoon. Had I kept her at home Jennifer would still be alive."

I unceremoniously thrust the flowers into the hard stainless steel holder. The grave became my indictment. Suddenly I was cold.

I left the graveyard as quickly as I could, stumbling, sliding with Victoria down the small incline with its loosened bracken, turning with one last glance behind me at the flowers on her lonely grave. Throwing all the cleaning tools and trimmings into the boot of my car, I drove home with these thoughts, imprisoning within me a hijacked future of self-blame and self-hatred.

Driving home I encountered children spilling out from school, and I remembered how excitedly Jennifer would have been in their number. Why did home seem so far away?

I sat in our living room. Nothing could ever bring me comfort again. I was overwhelmed, and I knew only one thing: I could not go on.

In the middle of our living room, in the middle of tears and pain, something began to stir within me, something that did not seem right, something that left a bad taste. This would not be the only time I would be aware of this. I can now say that the Evil One takes every opportunity to slay us. Sometimes we are easy game – but be aware of bad taste! God gives none of it to His children. So I prayed, calling to the only One whom I knew could help me. Not knowing what else to do, I opened my Bible, asking and trusting Him to speak to me. When God is our Father, we can come to Him as we are, however distraught. I made my dire need known to Him. He sat with me. All I could do was open my Bible. I did not open to this verse, somehow this verse opened to me: "Then Eli perceived that the LORD had called the boy" (1 Samuel 3:8).

God was telling Eli that He had called Samuel, and not Eli. I too was to understand that God had called Jennifer, who was my child. My condemnation was gone. I was blameless. I was free! The Evil One is a liar. His accusing thoughts will always leave a bad taste in our souls, evil thoughts, such as he had just thrown upon me own his evil darkness, but God's words own His truth, His love and His gentleness. Jesus, in my quietness and in my need, spoke life to my heart, comforting me with the truth that in His hands alone are life and death. The Lord "had called the boy". I was not to carry the guilt of it. Again He embraced me. He lifted me out of the mire, and set my feet upon the Rock.

12

"MUMMY, TELL ME MORE ABOUT HEAVEN"

Life became more unliveable, while death held more attraction. My days battled such thinking, and yes, God was holding me, but nights were always hard.

I became more disturbed that because Jennifer had been only nine years old, and because she had died alone in such frightening circumstances, she entered an eternity for which she was unprepared. Of course I underlie the beautiful reality of heaven, the joy of a great Saviour. Given the option, however, I had no doubt she would have wanted to live her life within her family. Her murderer had deprived her of this. I prayed to know if she was happy. Don't we find personal answers elusive? No one wrote the Bible with our names in it, and the more I searched, the more I found myself without the answers.

Death, in every respect, is a tragedy. We are eternal beings. I thought back to Eve and wondered how she and Adam had ever managed to come to terms with the death and loss of Abel their son. On the death of this young man, solemnly unparalleled, nothing could have assuaged their grief. Neither knew anything of the pain of death, nor its cruel finality. I wondered how they coped, perhaps they never saw Cain again either. I felt for them, now with a new understanding.

What about heaven, where is it, what's it all about? God seems to be singularly evasive here. All I could read in the Scriptures was what was not in heaven, and while it was wonderful to know of no more sorrow, sickness, sin, even no more battles, I needed to know more. I thought of Jennifer so much, and how she delighted so often to ask and hear more of heaven. I made my search more intensive.

Shall we know each other in heaven? This was my first serious question. I genuinely thought heaven would fail me here. Perhaps we may never again interact with one another in our personal relationships and the love we have shared. In this I was wrong and how glad I was to be wrong.

I searched to find the truth I needed. After some time digging, God did show me, and He brought me to unfamiliar words, relating to our early patriarchs. They were "gathered to their people". We read their stories in Genesis and Exodus. I understood as I read such words, either they went in spirit immediately upon their death, to be with their own loved ones, or their bodily remains were to be buried in the same ground. I supposed it to be the latter.

Moses made the difference. Aaron, his older brother, had been told to climb Mount Hor where he would die, and it was said there of him that "Aaron shall be gathered to his people" (Numbers 20:26). On Moses' own death, he was told to climb Mount Nebo. Here he climbed alone, and here he died alone, and here God spoke the same words. God, alone on the top of the mountain buried Moses' body. But "no one knows his grave to this day" (Deuteronomy 34:6).

In order to be gathered to his people Moses himself must be taken and reunited with those of his own who had gone before. Such truth hit my sorry mind like a flash of a torch in the darkness. God's tenderness engaged my heart while He showed me that we really are gathered to those we love.

I again began to search for myself, this time praying for something more personal.

God loves to surprise us. He surprised me in showing me two people about whom I was reading. One was Paul, the apostle; the other, again, was Moses. Paul? I have come to love him, though I think he suffers from a bad press. Were we without this man's revelation, his humility, we would remain impoverished. Paul has been called a letter writer extraordinaire! I reckon his finest to be that sent to the Romans, and never tire of reading such a revelation of grace – we have much to learn. Even the apostle Peter said that he found it difficult. But Paul loved to share.

To the people of Corinth, a prosperous town in Greece where he ministered and established a church, he wrote two recorded letters. These people gave him a bit of a hard time, and in his second letter, Paul did not mince words. This man used no unnecessary tact when his apostleship and leadership were impugned by a haughty "don't tell me what to do" people. And it was here I saw something even more wonderful. Paul recounted a time when he was taken up into heaven – as he describes, to the third heaven.

My thought was this. If God would do this for Paul, He can and He would do the same for me. I remembered it was Paul who said, "for He who worked effectively in Peter for the apostleship to the circumcised also worked effectively in me" (Galatians 2:8).

The same powerful Spirit works in all Christians. This is grace, as Paul delights to tell.

I had also been reading, at the same time, this prayer of Moses. "Please, show me Your glory" (Exodus 33:18).

God answered his prayer too.

So I stood in their shoes and prayed their prayer. I had the same hunger and I had the same God.

"Lord, what You have done for Moses and for Paul, I ask You to do for me. Please show me Jennifer as she is in glory, show me that she is the same happy child, please show me she is glad to be where she is. You know that I have done all that I can do to find this out."

I honestly think we gladden God's heart when we delight to take another step of faith, "to Him who is able to do exceedingly abundantly above all that we ask or think" (Ephesians 3:20).

The dark sea where He brought me was cold, and daunting. I did not know it was a dream as I stood there that night like "a stranger on the shore". It was not where I wished to be. I have a fear of water, but my eyes had fastened upon the most prestigious shining white liner I had ever seen, anchored on the far horizon. Even at a distance, it was resplendent. I must reach that ship. I knew why, but I did not know how. With the fear of what I had to do, I stepped alone into those waters, a deep sea. I still feel the coldness of that sea as it flooded around and over my ankles and legs. The beautiful ship before me held my unbroken gaze and I walked towards it. My toes clenched the sand as far as I was able, darkness thickening its hold around me. I knew the sea would soon take me and, aware of this, I made myself move, with more determination. Somehow a metallic walkway was being positioned beneath my feet and I felt the safety and solidness of it, even as heavy waters heaved upon me. The walkway was holding me, though I did not know how, its solidity proving my safety.

I reached the side of the imposing liner. I'd made it. But how could I board? Conscious that I was here under false pretences, I felt furtive, like a stowaway. I could not make my way into the ship through its impressive entrance, but

I did so quietly through an unseen cargo area. I knew I was now in the passenger quarters, albeit mindful of an unnerving fear. But a grandeur enwrapped itself around me, bringing me a wonderful sense of belonging.

A tall man was approaching. This distinguished gentleman wearing an impeccable white naval uniform formally addressed me, "You are Pat. You are here to see Jennifer."

There was a tenderness with him, as if he knew my apprehension. Showing me to an adjacent room, he asked me to wait. I was alone. This is what I saw. The room itself held a regal aura, yet conveying nothing of discomfort, nor unease. Carpet and furnishings displayed no decayed elegance; they were refreshingly beautiful; the superb panelling around the room got my attention. Even before looking at it, the rich aroma confirmed it to be cedar. I knew I had got this from Andrew, a lover of wood.

A door opened further down the passageway and I quickly left the room, hearing laughter. As the door closed, I felt I had interrupted something exciting. The man was holding Jennifer's hand, bringing her to me.

My first look! She was still smiling that sparkled smile, and she was beautiful! We called simultaneously to one another, our voices broken,

"Mummy!"

"Jennifer!"

Dressed in the same clothes in which she had left that day, the clothes that she so loved, the white and red strawberry t-shirt, red corduroy trousers, she ran to me as

I did to her. About to touch and embrace one another, my dream was broken.

Yet my dream continued. We were now within the ship's galley. Instead of the expected small porthole, I saw a wide clear window shaped something like a huge kitchen hatchway. As I looked at what was happening, many people were coming to the hatch window. Some came alone, some in company, but all received a different supply of food. Interestingly, each given package was different. As they came to the open window so they left to return, holding tightly that which had been given to them. I knew they were going back to the place I too had just come from. Jennifer stood with me, watching.

Once again on the deck of the ship, I now knew it was time to leave, sadness holding me as I watched her.

I was not surprised to hear her say, in those soft little tones, "Mummy, you have to go back."

She spoke with a quiet conviction, her voice belying those earthly nine years. Now I knew this would be the last time I could be with her. Yes, I understood that I must leave, but there was one remaining thing so important to me, the one thing I was here to ask of her. I felt she knew what I was now about to say. For a few moments, we were silent as we looked at one another, knowing we would soon part.

I, too, quietly spoke.

"Jennifer, you can come back with me. There is a walkway, it's safe, it's easy."

"Mummy," her reply, again so soft, "I know that. But I'm 'asposed to stay here," that little Jennifer idiom so touchingly endearing. "But you go, Mummy, 'cos I'm coming back there. I'm coming back there again."

Then with a last engaging look, she left me. The ship's outer door thudded behind her as I stood alone, remembering another day and another door as it too closed behind her. With pain I ran to the steel door calling her name, my hand sore as I hammered upon it. I know I will never forget her love that I felt right then. Jennifer had remained at the door, unseen, to say these words.

"Mummy, I'm still here."

Just as one would respond to a little child, so Jennifer lovingly, though unseen, said to me, "Mummy, I'm still here! You go back!"

The smile was in her voice.

She left me, and my heart stopped dancing. But this time I smiled. This time she returned to her beautiful place, with no more hurt, and no more pain. Here she had no more need to ask the questions she had never tired of asking.

"Mummy, tell me more about heaven."

Jesus said, "I go to prepare a place for you" (John 14:2). I take this opportunity to stress those last two very personal words.

Dreams – they are never known for pulling their punches. This one brought me again to where I did not expect to be. God knows His own business. Somehow, I arrived where I had started. The sea, still in its darkness, gushed behind me. My return to normality held a very different scenario. There was nothing familiar here. Sleeping Beauty in her fairy tale had been unaware of the ravaging neglect of the beauty of her castle and the gardens of her heritage. When she awoke she saw all that had once been beautiful now changed to an overgrown world of darkness, decay and death. I, too, was being shown – with new eyes – what had evidently been a beautiful world.

My first impression was that of sinister gloom, of beauty lost, with the replacement of a wearisome struggle. Trees, flora, fauna, vegetation, all their lush greenery had lost its gladness. Looking around I tried to make my way through this strong, unwieldy tangle of darkness, pulling back thorns and briars; at times needing to use the sharp knife that had been placed in my hand. As I did, I saw people around me slipping and slithering, falling into their own darkness, their own dirt, never to either regain nor retain their steps. As they constantly fell, I was also aware how they never seemed surprised. They got up, to unwittingly fall again, becoming even more engrained with dirt. But there was one thing I had not been aware of. Surely this was the reason I was being shown such things.

While these dear people walked in darkness, I walked in light. I had been wearing a form of miner's helmet. Everywhere I turned, I could clearly see around me. Then I saw others wearing these same helmets with the same intrinsic light. But I watched those walking in darkness, still struggling, still slithering, still painfully falling in more mud, never aware of where their road was leading them.

Jesus said these words, "I am the light of the world. He who follows Me shall not walk in darkness, but have the light of life" (John 8:12). Proverbs tells us this, "the path of the just is like the shining sun, that shines ever brighter unto the perfect day. The way of the wicked is like darkness; they do not know what makes them stumble" (Proverbs 4:18–19).

As I watched all of this before me, my heart welled up with a compassion I knew was not my own. That night I believe God exchanged His gracious heart for my unfeeling one. Thirty years would pass when I would, in a courtroom, remember this dream. It was there I watched a depraved, darkened man, only this time I watched not only with a pain that crushed me, but a compassion that held me.

Nothing can justify the love of God, and neither can any be deserving of it. It is the reason God delights in it. Grace is a strange word for us, yet it is here that we do God a great injustice. This is grace – the desire of God doing for each of us all that we cannot do for ourselves and we take it on the cost at which it was gained. God never said that sin didn't matter. He showed us the price that had to be paid. He also told what it has got for us. The apostle Paul put it this way, "we have access by faith into this grace in which we stand" (Romans 5:2). God wants us to know that His grace is real, and it is available. Like those with light, we will stand. Like those in darkness, none can stand. This is the power of sin in every life. We will stand only in that which He has done for us. We have it when we need it, and we take it by faith.

13

BATTLES WHICH MUST BE WON!

Unfortunately, these were always things which I could not share with Andrew. He had not yet come to salvation, the wonderment of knowing God, having forgiveness and peace. How much I prayed for him only God knows. Cyril, his father, lived this with me. Saved when Andrew was just a year old, Granda grew to love the Lord in an amazing way, and I found his fellowship over those years to be rich. As we both continued to call upon God for his salvation, years were passing with Andrew still reluctant to deal with it. Of course, he knew he must do at some time, but it was always something to be dealt with in the future. Having an unsaved spouse is a lonely faith. It had become uncomfortable for us both to have a serious conversation but I did find this understandable. No one finds baring their soul easy, and though we could often talk of these things while in company, I learned to leave it with Him. God was teaching me.

Over time, however, I began to sense a growing conviction that God was working in Andrew. This is actually a wonderful thing, as God addresses our need of Him. We will never feel comfortable when God ministers to us in such a personal way but the Holy Spirit knows His business. The prime intention of Satan is to deceive. He stands against the salvation of God.

"But even if our gospel is veiled, it is veiled to those who are perishing, whose minds the god of this age has blinded, who do not believe, lest the light of the gospel of the glory of Christ, who is the image of God, should shine on them" (2 Corinthians 4:3–4).

While I was thankful to God for Andrew and his support, there came a time when things were coming to such a head that I felt I had gone as far as I could go. While the Evil One sneeringly continued to make my life difficult, I had to acknowledge before my Father that I could not go on. My prayer was specific.

"Lord, I say to you that I cannot go on."

I was under no illusion that I must spell things out to Him. I knew that He knew.

"I ask you now that Andrew within the next two years will be saved. After that I can pray no more."

It was done. My prayer that night still registers its gravity and earnestness until this day. Something was about to happen shortly, confirming God's agreement.

My daily reading had taken me to Matthew's gospel. Don't we tend to read things in the Scriptures with slovenly familiarity? In reading the same words so often I think we can miss what the Holy Spirit wishes to reveal to us. I was reading Matthew chapter 11 and came to a formidable statement, words which I had never taken with personal importance. However, the weight of my business with God regarding Andrew was uppermost as I searched Him out. These words came to me with eye-opening clarity.

"[T]he kingdom of heaven suffers violence, and the violent take it by force" (Matthew 11:12).

In other words, "Fight for it!"

This Kingdom was mine. I was told to bring a new violence before the very gates of heaven, upon all the promises that God had given me; not with violence against God, but a violence upon the Word and the will of God. Faith is never passive, and must always stand upon His Word. Therefore it is a fight and we are told it is always a "good fight"(1 Timothy 6:12).

Some months of Kingdom-grasping passed when one Sunday morning at church the man who had been preaching left these final words with us, "Why don't you step out in faith and ask someone you care about to come with you tonight?"

Andrew had often made it clear not to ask him to church, and I accepted this with understanding. Victoria, or either of the boys, would ask him to come for some things they were involved in, and in this he gladly relented.

This September evening we were alone, and again in bathroom quietness, I entrusted this to God. Andrew, when asked, not only came willingly with me that night but did so for the next two years. How amazing is that?

A year had passed, and Andrew had been coming with me every Sunday evening. I had been in this church for some years, and found its fellowship warm and caring. I missed my former church but always managed to keep in touch. Their prayers for us were faithful. Andrew, or Andy as he was known, loved people and his camaraderie, and humour, engaged warmly with them. All the while I was still violently taking the Kingdom by prayer as I learnt to own God's Word and know His heart.

September had come round again. As Andrew loves walking, he had arranged to take a few days off to go to the mountains. This time he went alone to walk through the Blue Stack Mountains in Co. Donegal. Granda, with Grannie, Victoria and I, drove him to the drop-off point and watched as he happily set off with the prescribed rucksack. We had arranged to pick him up at Falcarragh in two days, a small town on the north Atlantic coast, on the Sunday evening.

Somehow, I knew that the Lord had plans to meet with him. Each night I prayed for a real encounter, particularly that last Saturday night. Over the weekend, the weather had become treacherous, even quite violent. Although Andrew is an experienced walker and climber, I was concerned for him that night, and prayed for his protection. It could not be easy for him. We set off early the next morning heading north west through what had now become torrential rain, having to stop the car on several occasions. Even in Ireland this was proving difficult. The weather continued to worsen.

But behind the scenes, God was again doing His own business. Andrew told me the details later, and he makes this a key issue to his salvation. That Saturday evening he had to pitch his tent without being able to take the bearings that he needed, hoping for a better opportunity the next morning. But in fact the next morning had become worse. Strong wind and rain at horizontal level had become too strong for him to identify any placement, nor was it possible to see landmarks. The compass was useless. He knew he had to meet us at a certain time, at a place he then had no idea how to reach. For the first time Andrew was afraid. In sharing his testimony, he does say that perhaps the Lord heightened that fear, but then, perhaps not. This was his reality. He prayed. For Andrew, there came a day.

"Lord I ask You now to help me. If You bring me to Falcarragh for the time agreed, I will continue to attend church until the day You save me, or I reject You."

At that point, he did the only thing he knowingly could do. He set his compass setting to north. Without needful bearings, he made his way forward.

At the exact place and exact time arranged, we met. Victoria's words said it all as we watched him walk the short uphill distance towards us.

"Mum, look at Dad. Why can he not walk properly?"

There he was. God had answered his prayer, and Andrew kept his promise. He was saved a year later at a gospel mission in our church. I knew on the last night of that mission that this was his desire, and when at home, I later left him alone and went to bed. I so believed, as he thought upon all these things that he had heard, that he would tell me he had trusted Jesus for his salvation. Before coming to bed, Andrew had indeed prayed a prayer of repentance, and he did trust, but to tell me was too hard for him. The devil loves to make it so. But Andrew remembered his sister telling him how she had asked God to confirm something very needful to her. Late that same Sunday night he prayed, "Lord I know you have saved me. I now need your assurance to me. Please give me a word when I come down in the morning from Pat's Bible (which sat in the kitchen) that You really have saved me."

The next morning alone, he opened my Bible, to this verse: "Sing to the LORD! Praise the LORD! For He has delivered the life of the poor from the hand of evildoers" (Jeremiah 20:13).

Still unable to tell me and others what he had done for two days, he finally brought, bravely I think, my Bible to me to read the above verses, and ask me what it meant. My reply was that it was obviously something good, which God had done for him since he should praise and sing about it. I waited to hear the words I had longed to hear and words I had prayed for, for over twenty-four years.

"Pat, I asked the Lord to save me on Sunday night, and I know now that He did."

So began a beautiful fellowship, a new time of sharing, a time of learning, and a time of rejoicing together. The date was 3rd November 1993. God had indeed heard my prayer those two years ago.

That night Andrew also told his father what he had done, and how God had answered and assured him.

I remember dear Granda lovingly saying to him, "Do you recall the paralysed man that Jesus healed when his friends lowered him through the roof? Jesus not only said these words, 'Son, your sins are forgiven,' but he also said, 'Arise, take up your bed and walk'" (Mark 2:5, 9). "Andrew, God not only forgives us, but gives us His ability to live it and walk it out."

Cyril died some years later. For the last ten years of his life, he and Grannie had lived with us in a newly built self-contained flat, adjoined to our house. Each morning he loved to take our two dogs walking over the fields, and when he opened our back kitchen door, he would ask the same question and I loved his smile, "Well, Pat, are you rejoicing?"

Then I would hear of the fellowship he had with Christ as he walked through the fields, and what he had been reading that morning. I valued those times, and also learned to bluff it on some occasions! I am sure he knew when I wasn't on the ball.

"Pat, Jesus is there to lean on," he would say.

I'm still so thankful that Andrew had come to know fellowship with his father in those six years before his father died. We learnt much from Cyril and loved his heartening encouragement not only to us but also to all the family. I will always remember his characteristic words to anyone in trouble, "Och, brother, God's not dead yet."

And that's the God we've got. Let's learn to fight!

14

DAYS CLOSING IN

"Andy, Pat, you need closure. You know we pray for this."

While appreciating their concern for us, we knew that few people could realise the dread we harboured.

Over the years as a family, we had brought ourselves to accept Jennifer's death. The knowledge that one day we would see her again, and one day would be with her for ever, proved great comfort to us all, but that day of reunion seemed so unreachable, trapped in some distant future.

Were we to find this closure, we must then see the face of her killer. We must set our eyes on the last human face Jennifer was ever to see, as we would learn more of the suffering and the fear that were hers in those final hours. We hoped never to be brought to this. I wondered if there might be mitigating excuses presented at the trial for this man's culpability. Would we hear something of a neglectful, abusive upbringing?

Whatever we would have to come through, we steeled ourselves to face a situation more harrowing than we could bear. All of this played its part in our dread of what was termed "closure".

Less than one year after the murder of Jennifer, a news report on national TV declared what was happening to another family, this time in Scotland. Horror of what had just happened to their daughter again became our own.

Stunned to hear of another young girl abducted not far from her home in Coldstream in the Scottish Borders, we personally felt that pain wrenching us again. Susan Maxwell was eleven years old, cycling home from an afternoon of tennis on a summer's day in July 1982. It was the first time on her own. Susan lived far away from Ballinderry, yet somehow I knew this must be the same man! Two weeks passed before Susan's decomposed body was found behind a layby in the English Midlands, her underwear removed. To me it appeared too similar to be coincidental.

The trial against Robert Black would take place for Jennifer's murder thirty years later upon what is now known as Similar Fact Evidence. The police investigation team were encouraged when I told them how I had always taken this to be the work of the same man. The likeness of this second murder was almost identical. I did not know, at the time of the abduction and the finding of Jennifer's body, our own Chief Constable had been in touch with the police regarding the enquiry of

Genette Tate in 1978 in England, having himself noted the similarity. The sad fact remains that Genette's body is still unrecovered.

The itinerant paedophile, however, was far from having finished his business.

It was July 1983, one year following Susan Maxwell's murder. A five-year-old girl, Caroline Hogg, also went missing, this time from a seafront promenade in Portobello, Scotland. Caroline had been at a birthday party that afternoon, still wearing her party dress, when she had been allowed to stay out for a few minutes longer. Within a short while, when called and then searched for, it seemed she too had vanished. One of the last sightings of Caroline described her being led away, her hand in the grip of a man, her little face tightened with anxiety. Caroline's body was found ten days later in a ditch, again in the English Midlands; her underwear also removed.

"Something is happening here," I thought. But how can one man be responsible for all four murders?

While I believed this to be the same man, I wondered how he could be in all of these places. There were prevailing similarities. Could four men have done the same sordid crime in similar manner throughout the British Isles? In 1983, no one had heard of Robert Black. Very few crimes of this nature had been committed in the UK, and the tortuous murders of little girls shocked the whole of the nation. There was now a new shame within British society that such a villain could so neatly hide himself amongst us.

Less than three years later, in March 1986, ten-year-old Sarah Jayne Harper disappeared, this time from Morley near Leeds. Like ourselves, her searching parents agonised for three-and-a-half weeks. The River Trent in Nottingham revealed her young body. She had suffered serious sexual assault; a fifth murdered child within almost eight years.

Sarah had left home to go only 200 yards on a wet Wednesday evening to the corner shop to buy a loaf of bread for her mother. She reached the shop and was seen returning home. Within that short time, that short distance, no one ever saw her alive again. Our hearts reeled as we learnt of these ongoing tragedies and I knew there must be something that had to connect them. The term Similar Fact Evidence would take another twenty-five years before being brought into court trials with the weight it was worthy of.

Teresa Thornhill's height belied her age, being four foot eleven inches tall, giving an impression of her being younger. In April 1988, Teresa suffered an attempt by the driver of a van to abduct her. She was fifteen years old, but able to give the most arduous fight needed for her life. When on her last legs, her friend, a boy whom she had just left, ran back hearing her screams. The two young people struggled to fight him off. Robert Black made his getaway. That evening he drove off empty-handed in an empty van, leaving, for the first time, one of his victims alive. Teresa had escaped. The court sentenced Robert Black for her attempted abduction at his trial in Newcastle-upon-Tyne in 1994. Many times, I have thought of Teresa, and wondered about the personal repercussions of this attempt upon her young life.

She spoke of this harrowing event twenty-three years later, in an ITV interview on the day of the murderer's guilty verdict in Northern Ireland. The ordeal had left its mark, "People look at me and they think, 'Oh that's the girl that survived, she looks okay.' But inside to be honest I'm suffering. I feel like there is something missing from my life that was taken from me. And I just can't find what it is. I sometimes feel so guilty, you know, because I'm here and they're not."

She continued to say that, as a consequence, she has become overprotective of her two sons. Why should this lovely, innocent girl bring condemnation upon herself in being alive while others were not so fortunate? My heart goes out to her. I do hope one day that she will read these words from our family, "Teresa, you are alive. We have no answers, no adequate answers, to what are unanswerable questions, but you are alive. Please, just be glad. And, please, Teresa, never be ashamed to live out your gladness."

Two years after Teresa's attempted abduction something significant was to take place to a retired gentleman working in his garden on a quiet weekend in the small town of Stow; the repercussions of which were to have a momentous effect upon many, not least upon ourselves.

15

BLACK'S DARK DAY

Andrew and I have driven through the Scottish Borders on many occasions, finding their localities so alike to our own quietly rural Ulster towns and villages, "where everybody knows your name".

David Herkes' garden, from the roadside, fell on a downward incline, causing him to be virtually unnoticed by vehicles or passers-by, particularly from the opposite side of the road. However, a white Transit van parked opposite was not unnoticed by him, and he found it strange to see the driver of the van beginning to use a grimy rag to clean the outside of his windscreen. David was also aware of the little six-year-old girl who lived a short distance from him walking towards the van on that same far side of the road. How much, we should ask, could this have been incidental? For the people, and for the children of the UK, God, I think, had had enough.

Passing the van, her little sock-sandalled feet were all that was visible to him, but his eyes were taking a more sharpened scrutiny. He saw that she was not alone, adult feet standing with her, appearing at the roadside door. The little feet were unseen, while the van driver started the motor of his van and engaged a fast three-point-turn. David looked along the footpath where she had been. It's empty! She's gone! Where was the little girl? The six-year-old child that he knew so well had just disappeared. The white van had gone! There was nothing, no one there. David Herkes had just witnessed a child abduction!

I often wonder in those blood-draining seconds how hard it must have been for this man to make what he had just witnessed in any way plausible to his benumbed mind.

He was able, with acute presence of mind, to take the registration number of the van and to call the girl's mother. Let's not forget this was before the use of mobile phones. He then ran the short distance to the nearby police station. A search urgently under way, all traffic was stopped and questioned in regard to the van, crucial time all too quickly escaping. Had he got away? One of the drivers questioned as he drove through confirmed he had seen that van parked in a layby two miles north. What had taken his attention was that he had seen the driver getting out of the van. Nothing unusual in that, but something in his demeanour, his body undressed apart from trousers, had left him with a sinister impression.

That Saturday, unusually for Stow, quite a few police cars were already in the vicinity, quickly converging at the site of the abduction, contemplating an urgent plan of action.

Something was again about to happen.

David Herkes was standing in the street with the girl's parents. Her father himself was a policeman, and on duty that day. Suddenly this man who had seen the child abducted, had fastened his eyes on one white van now, incredibly, approaching the checkpoint.

"That's him," David's voice shrieked. "He's coming … that's him, that's the man!"

In all seeming innocence, the same van was indeed approaching the police checkpoint; the number plate recognised. With nowhere to turn and nowhere to hide, the driver was trapped. This same van driver who had driven little children without mercy to where he wanted to take them, drove as a lamb to his own slaughter.

I am writing with dearth of words to describe the next few minutes. Her father ran before the oncoming skidding van. Wrenching the rear doors apart while Black was restrained, he entered its darkened interior, calling his daughter's name. The van was empty. Despair, fear, did the work of overcoming this dear man. He turned to leave. As he looked one final time behind him, he suddenly witnessed a small movement, an unrepeated quiet movement, under a pile of items strewn in the corner of the van. He heard no noise, nor saw any further movement, but he ran to that pile of rags.

Her father had found his little daughter … releasing her, she was barely alive. He found his little six-year-old thrust head first within an enclosed sleeping bag, arms tethered behind her, her mouth and face tightly gagged. This movement, that he had barely seen, from such a feeble child must have summoned her utmost mettle. Under medical prognosis she had fifteen, perhaps twenty minutes to live. We dare not guess what may have happened to her. On behalf of writer and reader alike, I take this opportunity to applaud her.

The words of her father were amazingly controlled, and were a credit to the force he served, "That's my daughter, you b*****d!"

She had been sexually assaulted; her shoes, her socks removed.

Neither Andrew nor I shall ever forget the recorded words Robert Black spoke when he was arrested. Those words, given as evidence in Armagh Crown Court, "I knew I should have done this yesterday. Yesterday was Friday the thirteenth!" His strangely-loosened tongue denied the fact that Robert Black, for the next twenty-one years, would be known for his tight-lipped guile. But further remarks from Black were noted that day.

He said, "This was the day the roof caved in" speaking of having a "sudden rush of blood" when he first saw her walking on the pavement, and that he "had always liked little girls" and "just touched her a little". He also said that he wanted to take her somewhere like Blackpool, "to spend more time with her".

It appeared that he had left the layby having spent two hours with her, to be at his next delivery appointment in Galashiels, not so far away. How, and so we all may ask, could any man contemplate doing his daily business with a tethered, abused child who was barely alive hidden within his van, with stated intentions of doing worse! I seek no words for being wordless.

The later statement given from this little girl shows endearing innocence as she says that, when walking home that day from her friend's house, she saw Black standing at the open passenger door of his van.

"He wasn't looking at me then, but then he looked at me. I didn't know he was a bad man then. He said, 'Sorry,' but then he grabbed me around the waist and pushed me under the chair of the van."

Retired Lothian and Borders Detective Chief Superintendent Roger Orr, told the court in 2011 how Black, when he took her, twice shouted at the girl to be quiet, as he calmly reversed thirty yards down the road, performed a three-point-turn and drove out of the village.

A short time later it was brought to police attention that the same man had earlier stopped to ask directions from a twelve-year-old girl. She had been walking her dog. Unnoticed by Black the dog was exploring a nearby field, but made its presence known as it bounded up to her side, thus securing her safety. Black made his escape.

I think it safe to say that the large pet retriever unwittingly saved this young girl's life.

Deputy Chief Constable Hector Clark, accompanied by Detective Superintendent Andrew Watt reached the quiet police station of Selkirk on Monday 16th July.

I quote from Mr Clark's own words, "Without any formalities the sergeant took us two visitors through the back of the office to the cells. We stood quietly in the corridor as the door was unlocked. The sergeant stood back to allow Andrew and me in.

"Two things struck me immediately. The first was that the man we had come to see could only be described as scruffy, and, secondly, he smelled. It was a smell and a feeling that immediately carried me back to Portobello and the start of the journey in 1983 that had today seven years later, led to this cell. It was a cell more used to housing Saturday night drunks than criminals of the notoriety I suspected Mr Black was about to achieve.

"Apart from the smell of him, Black was, by anyone's view, scruffy. His hair was unkempt and greasy, his beard bushy and tangled. His clothes were tattered. He could easily be a tramp taken off the streets and put into the cells."

Mr David Herkes later received meritorious awards by Lothian and Borders Police, and separate awards proffered by the Police Federation. Our family add our gifting and gratitude to this dear man.

Robert Black had abducted, and abused his last little victim.

16

DAYS CLOSING IN

Born in 1947 to a single mother, Robert Black became a foster child to a couple in their fifties. Both having died before he was eleven, he was sent to a children's home in Falkirk. At the age of twelve, he was accused without charge of the attempted rape of a young girl. Placed at that time in an all boys' school in Musselburgh, he walked the short distance to Portobello, outside Edinburgh, from where many years later he abducted, abused and murdered little Caroline Hogg. Black loved swimming and worked as a lifeguard at Hornsey Road Baths, the local swimming pool. Authorities were quick to dismiss him when seen fondling small girls. He said in his later recorded interviews how he liked to watch little girls in their swimsuits.

When he was sixteen years old, he lured a seven-year-old girl to a disused air-raid shelter on the pretext of showing her some kittens. He sexually assaulted and strangled her until she lost consciousness, leaving her for dead. Eventually the little girl was found bleeding and in tears. Robert Black, however, was not imprisoned for this either. At the age of nineteen, while babysitting another seven-year-old girl, he received a Borstal sentence of one year for repeatedly violating her.

Later, Black worked as a van driver for a firm in London delivering advertising posters for billboards throughout the UK. Drivers for this firm would take batches of posters on regular routes, dropping them off with customers before returning to London. One of their vans was in regular use on runs to Northern Ireland.

After his trial and conviction in Newcastle in 1994, a new investigation for Jennifer's murder was opened. But after two years the Royal Ulster Constabulary was unable to make a legitimate case. It wasn't until 2003 that we first met with the new police team and, a year after that, Detective Chief Superintendent Raymond Murray had re-opened the case under the law of Similar Fact Evidence. This was a breakthrough.

The police team undertaking the inquiry arranged ongoing meetings with us away from media attention over the course of the next eight years and we established a great rapport with them. These men, Detective Chief Superintendent Raymond Murray, Detective Chief Inspector Stephen Clarke and Detective Constable Andy McLeod, impressed us with their diligence and their caring professionalism. Detective Chief Superintendent

Raymond Murray, whose father first worked on the case as a sergeant in 1981, described the enquiry over all those years as, "Bib and braces: nothing but good old-fashioned police work." Raymond and his team worked closely with us, keeping the family updated as they patiently, and indeed frustratingly, tried to piece together more and more evidence. It was good for us, but daunting to see the investigation progressing.

Had I been an outsider, I know I would have been glad for the family, that after thirty years there was an end drawing nigh, but I was growing more afraid. I sensed this upon us all as we tried again to put on a brave face. Hearing that Robert Black had suffered a stroke in prison, I cushioned myself with a way out. Maybe he would die. After all, he would never be free again. This I could share with very few. During the years before the trial, we prayed a lot, taking solace in the fact that our Father knew where we were at, and how we were hurting. It was so good to have Andrew with me in this, both of us feeling vulnerable and unable, yet trusting an able God.

It was good, too, to have our family involved with us in these continuous investigations and it brought us great comfort, giving renewed strength with shared commitment. Mark, now married to Jane with two children, was, at the time of the trial, forty-three years old. Philip was thirty-six, married to Susan, with a son. Victoria was thirty, soon to be married to (another) Andy. For Mark and Philip the ordeal of this trial would be both painful and distressing. Their memories of Jennifer, even after thirty years, will forever be part of them.

I also think of how much we appreciated Victoria. What I had not been conscious of, and I so wish I had been, was that she often felt herself on the outside, on some lonely periphery, never having her own personal memories of Jennifer. I do feel for her, but also think it has been good for her to grow without pain. I appreciated talking about this with her. Robert Black robbed Victoria of a beautiful sister. What we all went through together during the time of his trial has, I believe, in some measure addressed this.

Days continue to throw their stuff upon us. It was 2007. Susan, Philip's wife, was at last in hospital, in the maternity ward. We awaited the new little Cardy, but a watched phone refused to ring. This child would be their first. I had already rung Philip and told him I would wait for his call. There it was! At last! But why was his voice so choked?

"Mum, Susan had a little boy … I'm sorry Mum. The baby died."

Words and thoughts scrambled together within me as I stood trying to utter sympathy, or some kind of support. I tried to say something – but again words failed me.

Susan and Philip were to find that a streptococcal infection had invaded the birth canal. Little Phillip, given the utmost and urgent attention, did not survive, living only a few minutes. Susan also showed alarming physical repercussions; nursing care for her was amazing.

Unknown to us, Philip not only saw his little son die, but then watched, helplessly, his beloved wife suffer. Mercifully, Susan recovered. Once again, grief was overwhelming. We wonder why. But baby Phillip's Mum and Dad were Christians and his funeral service was touching. This beautiful song was sung, and bears well to them:

"Blessed be Your name
On the road marked with suffering
Though there's pain in the offering
Blessed be Your Name."[3]

It has become the testimony of many.

Some years before, I had innocently switched the television on, finding the beginning of a broadcast. I was ironing in our kitchen, and was surprised to find the introduction was highlighting an interview with the parents of murdered children. My first thought was to switch the television off, knowing they would be sharing the deep pain of which I was all too familiar, and I thought giving attention to ironing family laundry should be more urgent! The television remote control however was out of reach, and I quickly tried to finish my task, viewing only for a short while. The programme kept my attention, but left me with unforeseen tears.

---

[3] Extract taken from the song Cornerstone by Edward Mote, Reuben Morgan, Jonas Myrin and Eric Liljero . Copyright © 2002 Thankyou Music (PRS) (adm. worldwide at CapitolCMGPublishing.com excluding Europe which is adm. by Integrity Music, part of the David C Cook family. Songs@integritymusic.com) All rights reserved.

I had been watching families who couldn't make it. Some had been battling for years with deep depression, some trying to live with daily soul-destroying bitterness, some had withheld their children from having any life of freedom, and most had been unable to hold their marriage together. As I struggled in my kitchen to fold the ironing board, I watched these dear people baring their hearts, baring their lives; their faces showing a continuing grief that had blighted them. My face depicted their own hot tears.

It was then that the reality of what God had done for our own family throughout all these years took me aback. We too suffered the same pain they had just related, nor were we different from these dear but dreaded people I had just seen and heard in the trauma they had to come through. The difference was that we had been lifted. We had been held within strong arms. In those moments, I felt like the unworthy recipient of a traitor's pardon. God had held us together in ways I was naively unaware. It is worth knowing we have such a God who does not mind if we are ignorant of the depths of His love and touching concern for us within all of our dark days. He has determined to put us at the mercy of none of them. He proved that day how beautifully able He was for us all. I cried.

We now entered this collectively: but I had to learn something. The Lord, who had proved such enabling, was soon to lift me to new ground, uncomfortable new ground. As the deliberations for the trial were progressing, I so much more needed Him. While I fellowshipped in prayer, daily spending time with Him in His Word, one thing was becoming clearer. God was being God.

My eyes began to focus on the solemnity of God's justice. At first, I tried to take this to myself in some impersonal way, pushing aside verses that spoke of His justice much more clearly. His call to bring Robert Black to human accountability was being set before me as I read the Scriptures given to me. I did not care to know this; timidly wanting God to ignore what He was now telling me. We could not face seeing nor hearing this man.

Sometimes God encounters us when we neither ask nor expect. We want to escape the hard stuff. One morning, with the trial in mind, my usual reading plan had brought me to Psalm 9, where this verse caught my heart, "When He avenges blood, He remembers them; He does not forget the cry of the humble" (Psalm 9:12). It is God who seeks an accounting for bloodshed. He wanted me to know that He was not only doing this for His own righteous heart, but He was doing it for Jennifer. He does not forget the cry of the afflicted. I felt again His love holding me, and I loved Him for it.

I look at that Psalm in my Bible today and cannot fail to notice that not only did I underline it, but wrote the date beside it, reminding me of how unforgettably the Lord speaks. Unknown to us then, the trial would be underway within two years. God was telling me He would arrange all things needed for Black's accountability. We would no longer baulk at this; we would walk as a family, through more hard days.

17

THE DAY THE ASS
OPENED ITS MOUTH

The man would soon arrive, brought from Wakefield Prison in England, to Lisburn to answer the charge of the abduction and murder of Jennifer – guilty or not guilty. The Court House being beside his office and workplace, Andrew's emotions were strained as he watched the unfolding scenario that morning. While television cameras were being set up together with other media, he was not surprised to see the many passing school students take their time to stop with one another, pointing out these rare proceedings, while still aware of their scramble to get to school on time.

Our police team ensured we knew the gravity of the situation, and we expected their call informing us of Black's response. Still undecided what we should do in relation to attending court, we had chosen not to be present that morning. Something quite remarkable was to occur in the office when Andrew was spending time alone with the Lord, asking for the needful guidance in this decision. We were both of the same mind in thinking we could not do it. He was reading in Luke's gospel, "Now when they bring you to the synagogues and magistrates and authorities, do not worry about how or what you should answer, or what you should say. For the Holy Spirit will teach you in that very hour what you ought to say" (Luke 12:11–12).

When the team arrived to tell that Black had pleaded "Not guilty", their main concern was to ask Andrew if we would reconsider future court appearances. Andrew's reply was now unequivocal. He said "Yes."

It had never happened before, but that morning I had the same reading. Although for some reason, I had been disturbed and closed my Bible before I got to the place where Andrew had read. Therefore, when he told me that evening of what had transpired, I was so glad that God had spoken in this way to him. I was unaware that I too would hear these same words for myself, but we both knew that evening what we had to do.

The following day, thanking God for speaking to Andrew, and for the assurance we had both been given, I continued my own reading, then becoming amazed when the same words were now given to me. God had brought us each the assurance needed that He would not only be very close to us on these occasions, but the

Holy Spirit Himself would be our upholding. He would direct us in what to say, as and when we should. This proved to be true.

However, for Raymond and his team some eight years had been spent tediously doing the bib and braces stuff. From the earlier evidence, given in the 1994 trial in Newcastle, they knew the necessity at trial to establish proof of his presence in Northern Ireland on 12th August 1981. This was imperative; but it may have proved impossible. They aptly named this mind-numbing investigation, "Operation Perseverance".

So began the search into over 560,000 signed receipts, all on microfiche computer data, each going back for thirty years. In fact, the Robert Black files gave 187,000 individual references, together with 67,000 witness statements, and altogether 22 tonnes of documentation had amassed upon the case. Two articulated-lorries were required to transport the police files and exhibits from England to Northern Ireland together with hundreds of boxes relating to Black's past crimes. This was to fill one and a half secure storage rooms in Belfast. Amongst it all, they found the one thing they needed. A receipt.

Having found Black's dated signature on the back of it, together with a specified salary bonus on the same dates showing a delivery to Northern Ireland, the team were satisfied they had the proof of his presence here on the day of 12th August 1981.

In all of his interviews Black let nothing slip. He answered questions at Wakefield Prison under interrogation in 1996, on the abduction and murder of Jennifer, all to little or no avail. He seemed always to be six jumps ahead. Out of a score of ten, the inquisitors were proud to achieve three, possibly four.

In 2005, prison authorities transported him to HMP Maghaberry; a high security prison in Northern Ireland, only five miles from our home. Antrim, our country town, was the setting for his further interrogation. Great pains had been taken to refurbish Antrim Police Station, being the holding centre of many notorious offenders during the years of Ulster's ongoing troubles. The date for these proceedings, due to last three days, was set for 16th May 2005, Jennifer's birthday.

The interview strategy had taken more than a year to plan. Detective Chief Superintendent Murray had arranged for the clearance of the Antrim Serious Crime Suite complex to accommodate it. Nothing would be left undone and nothing left to chance; hence the arrival of Detective Constable Pamela Simpson. Pamela and those with her were highly-trained interrogative psychologists, familiar with all the taped recordings of Robert Black, and fully conversant with every conviction and with all his previous personal history.

Too quickly for comfort, the arranged Wednesday finally arrived. Alone that morning, I sensed Black's nearness. His evil seemed to leave an odour, as it encroached our home. I wondered how he was feeling as he remembered Jennifer again. Surely he harboured some untold regret, some secret remorse? I thought not, but hoped he was suffering, and I hoped his memories were painful. I thought too of the prison guards having to take Black to Antrim town, fifteen miles away, for his interrogation. They knew why he had been brought here.

He must talk, surely he would. Raymond and the team were less expectant – they thought they knew their man's professionalism, his proud muzzled tongue.

The phone call I made to Andrew gave new expectancy, new excitement, upon what God had just told me.

My prayer had been precise. "Lord … You must make this man talk. You are the only one who can." And my prayer was answered.

I lifted my Bible, reading only my next daily chapters, allowing God who was teaching me the power of His words, to do His own thing. I expected to come across some personal encouragement, but unknowingly was about to read of an evil mercenary prophet called Balaam.

This man was under the hire of an enemy king to curse the people of God, to have them killed and overthrown. Balaam was on the move to meet the king and it is evident that he was after the proposed rich reward. God Himself had told the prophet that no one could curse those that God had blessed – but money talks!

On his way to the king, the donkey he was riding suddenly saw an angel, his sword drawn, standing on the road ahead of them. I would defy anyone, man or beast, not to cower. The donkey diverted to a field, and Balaam, unaware of the angel's appearance, immediately struck the beast and led her back on their journey. The angel took another threatening stance in a pathway with a wall on both sides. As Balaam's foot painfully crushed against the wall, he struck the donkey again. When this happened for a third time with no room to turn, the donkey lay down on the ground beneath him as Balaam struck her again. "Then the LORD opened the mouth of the donkey" (Numbers 22:28).

With my eyes transfixed. I had my answer. I knew that not only would Black talk, he would talk a lot.

Thus my immediate call to Andrew. When the police later phoned him that morning, he guaranteed them a good outcome, an amazing one, as he told them what God had said to me. They wished this to be true but were somewhat slower to believe. The trial against Robert Black would now take a notable turn. In Antrim police barracks, a male interrogator first questioned Black but achieved no results. Enter Pamela. For some unknown reason Black dropped his core defences – he liked her. Little did he know that God was opening another ass's mouth.

He gave no confession. But when told of the finding of the signed Coventry petrol receipt and asked if he agreed this would prove his presence in Northern Ireland, his first answer was, "It looks like it." Upon more direct questioning Black then said, recorded on tape, "Yes."

He also spoke of his many fantasies of perverse sexual abuses upon young girls. A further lapse in his concentration was to describe where he used to look for these little girls. That was his biggest slip-up.

The description he gave of a rural road was the exact illustration of the place from which he had abducted Jennifer: much too explicit for a man who claimed he had never been there before.

Detective Chief Inspector Stephen Clark said, "Black would have always been thinking of how far he could go during interview. It appears that this time he went too far."

Raymond expected the usual three-out-of-ten, hoping for five. They achieved a nine.

The hearing brought to Belfast Crown Court on a cold February day in 2011, was set to prove the establishing and the allowance of Similar Fact Evidence in the trial of Robert Black. This would show that each crime perpetrated by the same offender would leave personal distinguishing marks. Legalised for court trials in 2004, everything hinged upon Judge Anthony Hart, who would oversee the case, to give his acceptance.

Court buildings, we soon found, are stark. They are cold and bleak. Of course, you expect they should be. They seem to love imposing haughty grandeur upon all who enter. Belfast High Court, to me, held a likeness to Grand Central Station in New York, but without the feel-good factor. With huge ceilings, marble floors, stately columns guarding all doorways, we were impressed. The only lifeline came in the coffee that was given to us from the café.

The judge was arrayed in designated formal wig, and red robes; I was conscious that this was no television drama. This court commanded respect and Judge Hart presiding accordingly. We had never been in a courtroom before, certainly not in a Crown Court. Our church, again, lovingly held us in prayer as they empathised with what we were to face. I remember arriving nervously with Andrew and our pastor, Jimmy Ritchie. We dreaded our first time seeing Robert Black in the flesh.

On meeting there with Raymond, Stephen and Andy, together with the lovely Yvonne, we soon found a new and engaging strength. Yvonne proved herself to be not only an experienced Liaison Officer, but someone who accompanied us throughout all the hearings, the trial itself, the conviction, the sentence, and subsequent appeal. Yvonne had a gentle understanding of our dread in what we were to see and hear, and as we came to know her over the next two years she also became a loving friend. She was never short of witty repartee to Andrew's teasing banter. She took us in hand, explaining all we needed to know, and her support left its mark.

Raymond introduced us to Mr Toby Hedworth QC. He had been Junior Prosecuting Counsel in the trial against Robert Black in Newcastle in 1994 where Black received his conviction for the three English murders and the one attempted abduction of Teresa Thornhill in Nottingham, after already having been sentenced for the abduction of the little girl in Stow. We knew his skill, though he pulled no punches as to how difficult this may become.

A tall man, Toby arrested me with an earnestness rarely seen. As I shook his hand, his eyes bore a connection with my own which said more than any spoken words between us. My heart warmed immediately to his unspoken resolve – to bring this man to justice!

His assistant was Miss Donna McColgan, since that time she has become a Queen's Counsel herself, and a judge. What impressed everyone in court was the grave spoken delivery of Mr Toby Hedworth, his speech carrying forceful solemnity.

Shown into the courtroom, the media already present, we took our places to the left, though asked to move to the right, behind a glass partition. There we waited. Robert Black arrived. Will I ever forget that first image as he sat in front of us behind the see-through panel? His appearance showed total nonchalance. We expected this. We were to see the same demeanour, the same face and his same rear view throughout the next two years, but we were content to hold this place when asked if we would prefer to move. Mr Black should know the child's mother and father were directly behind him.

The reality of Robert Black, knowing he was the killer of our daughter, knowing him to be the killer of those three little girls, set before us a cruel credibility. My gaze held his visage as he sat in front of me, inches from us both. At the former hearings, we had already seen his face on video. This became gut-wrenching. The man was real. I could not turn to look at Andrew on my left, though I yearned to do so. If I were to look at him, we would connect with our painful emotions. Maybe this would be too much for us?

His grey hair curled over a sweatshirt, somehow allowing Black an entitlement to appear ordinary, an entitlement to grow older. His appearance betrayed his years. My eyes were trapped on the man. He showed a singular tiredness, an older-ness, a wizened smaller-ness. For almost twenty years, he had already been behind prison bars. As I watched him, I became aware of something else. This man was our own age, and this fact presented yet another: the man was our own age when he killed her.

David Spens held his defence. Other Defence Counsellors had presented problems in their reluctance to do so. Black had chosen well. He was thoroughly, time-consumingly thorough, and as time progressed, we were to become well accustomed to him. Softly spoken, he examined and cross-examined every detail of law with acute precision.

It surprised most people that we did appreciate his defence, our thinking being that there should be no doubt in a given guilty conviction. Our prayer was for, not only a guilty conviction, but one with a unanimous jury decision. And so, if Black was to be convicted he must be ably defended. David Spens fulfilled all his requirements.

The hearing took several days, the result of which gave the full permission, with stipulated legalities, for Similar Fact Evidence to be deployed. The trial was set for the following September.

18

DARKENING DAYS

2011 would give us more than we had expected. A month before the start of that new year the premises of Richardson Cardy were ransacked, robbed and trashed. All that could be taken was taken.

At only thirty-eight years old, Jane, Mark's wife, was brought to hospital from work early in 2011, suffering from stroke similarities. This was worrying, but Jane recovered well.

Andrew's birthday, which falls on St Patrick's Day (with my own a month later) was celebrated. But Andrew, at the time, seemed to have contracted flu which suddenly and seriously zapped him. Andy Cardy is never ill, having walked, run and mountain climbed since I had known him. He had just made an excursion to the shops that Saturday to buy me a birthday present. But I was worried.

After two more days a doctor was called, and that morning I transported him to hospital, doing my utmost to slowly avoid all the cracks in the road. To see him in such unbearable pain I soon realised that an ambulance should have been called. Andrew typically chose the transport of my own car. He would be all right … he must be all right. I refused to entertain any other thought. Diagnosis at the hospital however was worse – the result was meningitis. Few visitors could attend. Those of us who did were garbed and gowned, head to toe. In this uniformed mode, we presented ourselves to the patient. He later told us that, in his drugged condition, we looked akin to aliens who were walking over his walls. Results from more tests then declared viral pneumonia. Known as "the silent killer", with no positive prognosis, we were almost overwhelmed.

Kept in a High Dependency Unit for some days, the hospital then phoned to tell me how extremely urgent the matter had become. An ambulance had transferred him at high siren-blaring speed to Intensive Care in Belfast Ulster Hospital. I had just received the news; only Victoria and I being at home together. In my alarm my one thought was the desperation of losing him. I did something as I prayed that I had never done before. I sang the words of Psalm 34 in the seasonal April quietness of our open back door, just between Jesus and me, owning those amazing words of God and allowing my heart to make its own music. Recently I had taught myself this psalm. That evening, I praised Him. My heart warmed in faith as I brought those words to the One who was able for every day of my life.

That night Victoria and I quickly drove to the large Ulster Hospital where their Intensive Care department had undergone complete renewal. It was after midnight as we walked our echoing way alone, overawed with the softly-hued neon lighting telling us wordlessly to be quiet. Exhibited around us every grey machine stood in its pomposity as though set there to display some kind of alien takeover. I wasn't ready for this. We couldn't find Andrew here. He didn't belong here. Victoria, also sensing this, made a softly whispered comment, engagingly apt, "Mum, we are now entering the Starship Enterprise!"

It was good to laugh, I needed it, and I loved her for it. Then we found him. Attached to things above, to things behind, and things more untraceable, he looked lonely and he looked weak. They had plugged his bed into what looked like something from a nuclear substation, a nurse adopting the needful part of physicist. But he was able to speak, and he did have some likeness to the man we loved, never losing that good humour, nor his familiar positivity as those days sped by. Praise the Lord, Andrew did make a full recovery, though it did take some scary time.

That same year threw more at us. The economic climate was not good, and in June our business hit bankruptcy. Andrew and I found ourselves with the princely sum of £200. We had nothing. All was gone. His heart broke the morning he called the staff and workers together to declare the sad state of play, creditors being paid, and all attempts made to keep the firm afloat. This business had functioned for almost forty years, and in 1994 Andrew had managed to buy his partner out after he, himself, had become a Christian, and moved on with Mark and Philip, who later became partners.

People were so good to us when least expected and when most needed. Suffice to say that God is an adequate provider. We received all we needed, when we needed it. Andrew sat each day at his solitary desk with his phone, from his early start in the morning with silence for company, never giving in to depression or surrender, but always trusting, and ever thankful.

"Be anxious for nothing, but in everything by prayer and supplication, with thanksgiving, let your requests be made known to God; and the peace of God, which surpasses all understanding, will guard your hearts and minds through Christ Jesus" (Philippians 4:6–7).

It has been thought that the thanksgiving here refers to denoting continual thanks for everything that God has done. Let us recognise that the subject here is that which makes us worry. We are told to thank Him because, as our God, it is He who is at our hand and it is He who will take care of our every concern. The peace He gives holds us. This peace we take by faith even before seeing any change in any circumstance.

19

TRYING DAYS

Time flies. Time sneaks up. Time, in fact, frogmarches all relentlessly to where we do or do not want to go. It came with its Gestapo presence to our home. From all that we had just come through, the question to ask was how would we, or could we, come through this? September 2011 brought no warmth to beckon us.

Wednesday, the week before the trial was to start in Armagh, God again gave me something unforeseen. Alone, it was again just Him and me. Jesus being big and great, me being wee and weak, as I simply and in faith asked for His Lordship within this trial. This is when Psalm 109 impacted me with a confidence over all future court proceedings with Robert Black. Although I did not know this psalm with any familiarity, I did know the stamp of His assurance.

"[L]et an accuser stand at his right hand. When he is judged, let him be found guilty" (Psalm 109:6–7). I had shared the verse with Andrew and it gave us feet to stand. Only God could then do what He did.

Audrey, a good friend, unaware of this, phoned me on the following Saturday morning. I was alone. Audrey was resolute.

"Pat, right now we're going on holiday, about to set off for the airport. Wilbert [her husband] is in the car. But I had to phone you. I've been thinking of you, praying for the coming trial. After I'd prayed this morning, what do you think I read? I know this is God's Word for you and Andy."

Then she read Psalm 109 verse 7 out loud.

Upon my telling her that God had given me this same verse three days earlier, we were wordless. This confirmation became the family bedrock, holding us during the many dark weeks to come. Black's conviction was affirmed.

22nd September 2011, the date for the trial had arrived. For some months, we had become accustomed to Belfast Crown Court so we had some disappointment when hearing that Armagh Crown Court would hold this trial. I suppose we expected it to take place in our capital city, it seemed worthy of such regard, and was certainly nearer to us. However, a noted Ulster criminal was to be tried in Belfast on that date. What ensued was the fact that we could not have been treated in Armagh in any better fashion. Here the Crown Court offered us a private family room away from media attention, which

Belfast was unable to do. We were to welcome this room as the haven it proved to be, a respite from what would become too much for us as court proceedings would continue. It also enabled us to spend time and talk privately together with all who could join us, including the police team. Each morning from a well-stocked fridge we packed hungry men's lunches, together with tea, coffee and needful niceties. Within a short time we would appreciate even more all that this room would mean to us.

A three-day earlier hearing in the nearby Craigavon Crown Court had been set up under Judge Ronald Weatherup to ascertain and oversee the presentation of Bad Character Evidence, as legalised in 2004. This would allow information to be given to the jury that Robert Black was not a man who had done a one-off crime, but one who had been for many years a serial child abuser, and killer. Judge Weatherup affirmed that, were the jury firstly to hear these facts, they would have grave bias for a guilty conviction. It was therefore shown necessary for prosecution to prove his presence in Northern Ireland on the date of abduction. This judge would oversee the complete trial. We warmed to him.

Yvonne had us well prepared. At the beginning of the trial, details would be shown on screen to the court from television newsreel, and we were warned of what this would entail. As a family, we were told it would be wise to leave the courtroom while some of these scenes, too emotional for us, were shown. We had never seen footage of Jennifer's body being removed from the dam. The jury had no choice, and with nine of the twelve jurors being female, I know the distress of what they witnessed. This jury over the next six weeks would suffer unforgettable grief as the trial of Robert Black continued. They would have to hear him voicing his sexual fantasies. These twelve reluctant sacrificial lambs, if I may so call them, earned our respect. Quite a few accepted counselling when the trial ended. I shall always remember their tears. Earlier we had watched as their names were called for jury duty, none aware of what they were being called to do. They looked so innocent, nine women, a few of them quite young, and three men. This is our practice to determine guilt. I consider it a laudable one.

Mr Toby Hedworth led the prosecution, introducing his case to the jury. He presented the photograph of Jennifer to the courtroom, taken on the day of the royal wedding two weeks before her abduction, then holding her new red bicycle with bright-eyed delight. She was dressed as she was on the day of her murder, her face conveying her happiness, her love of life, her gentle innocence. This is how Robert Black encountered her.

Toby turned towards the jury, and this will remain with me as being so thoughtful, so touching, so needful, "While we put before you all the facts of this case, let us never forget that this is a nine-year-old little girl we are considering. Her name is Jennifer."

I loved him for making her, not a name in a newspaper, nor the name upon a trial indictment, but as she was – a beautiful child.

Called to be the first witness, Andrew quickly gave my hand that assuring squeeze as I walked to take my place, Robert Black again sat in front of us. I knew he watched me. The questions asked of me were to re-live the day and the time Jennifer left her home, and to give a brief maternal description of her.

A witness box is a solitary place. There is something about the confines of a court where the face of the judge becomes the only one engaged with your own and little portrays reality.

Told by the judge to address the jury, I did so. Donna finished her interview and I was about to release a hidden, though well needful, sigh when Mr Spens, Defence Counsel, stood up to ask further questions of me. This was unexpected. He asked if she had been wearing her cardigan when she left. Taken aback I began to fluster, but on making a quick apology, I answered ably, aware that this may be somewhat contentious. She did have the item in her hand as she left, but had not been wearing it as she closed the door behind her. I could not specify if she was wearing the cardigan as she cycled from the house. Glad to be factual; it was good to sit down.

And so we watched Robert Black display his polished nonplussed demeanour, guarded by two police officers. He was less than a metre in front of us. The first photograph shown on screen was of Jennifer home when she first got her new bicycle, and how significant that she was wearing the clothes in this photograph which she had on that day he was to snatch her off the road. For the short time it took to show the recording of her body being taken out of the dam where he had tossed her, we had left the court (the only occasion we did so), and so we were later told that it was only when the video was shown that he showed anything that could be called emotion. He smirked.

I reckon, or hoped, the smirk may have showed his discomfort of a painful conscience. He gave no awareness of such, but I knew he owned his evil memories. A further six weeks of daily observing Black, impressed me with one disturbing fact: Robert Black held his secrets, he locked within him all his secrets of all his victims, still using such to serve his evil gratification.

Yvonne, our Liaison Officer, made a good chauffeur. Her company lifted us. Travel time would last most of an hour while we motored through the scenic apple blossom for which County Armagh is noted. We were glad too of Andrew's engaging chat. He ever tried to lift us, always able to introduce some well-appreciated lightness, commonly called Irish banter or craic, as we drove. On every journey to the courthouse, in more serious measure, we took the time to pray together, learning that by doing this, no day would crush us, nor overwhelm us. Each morning Victoria accompanied us, and so often would Mark and Philip, also our Pastor Jimmy. Friends and family who supported us on these occasions proved invaluable.

Mr Hedworth, after days of factual presentation, his witnesses always severely cross-examined, was able to ascertain to Judge Weatherup and the jury Black's presence in Northern Ireland on the 12th August 1981. None could be unimpressed with the detailed specifics of the police investigation. The jury also heard the entire Bad Character Evidence of Robert Black in all its gory detail. I felt for our jury. In their innocence and ignorance of what they were to hear, the court witnessed tears and pain. This family were about to enter that which we dreaded. No one within this court would find either strength or composure in the hearing of it.

Played in their entirety to the court and jury, the recorded interviews of interrogation at Wakefield Prison in 1996, and, more importantly, Antrim Police Station in 2005, brought the jury to request adjournment from the judge on several occasions. Judge Weatherup was aware of this need for all. The court heard of all the previous convictions from his youth, finally hearing of the guilty convictions of the three child abductions and murders in England, the one attempted abduction of Teresa Thornhill in Nottingham, and the final abduction and assault upon a six-year-old girl where police caught him red-handed, each conveyed in their horrific entirety. Black sat unruffled, unperturbed, drinking his glass of water, eyeing tears on faces before and around him. Details were graphic. They could not be otherwise.

Andrew and I had determined to be in court throughout it all. We would not have the media publishing details of which we ourselves would be ignorant. For the rest of the world to be aware of things which the family who loved her did not know, was not to be considered. We felt we owed this to Jennifer.

The interviews taken at Antrim Police Station were upsetting and so we felt the need to tell family and friends to stay away, the impact of such being too heart-rending for all who heard, especially to those who had known Jennifer. Unfortunately, the jury did not have that option, and I take this opportunity to all who may read these words, to convey my deepest admiration and respect.

Hearing his Scottish accent for the first time became sore to our ears. His accent gave him the credence of being an ordinary man! He should not have been. He was no ordinary man. He should have been different from anyone else. I do know how absurd that sounds. From the outset, I realised more of the horrendous and emotional difficulty our investigative services must undergo as they tirelessly try to uncover truths that are quite ghastly. All is not as it ever seems.

We learned to steel ourselves as we listened to a man freely voice his perverted and depraved sexual fantasies. This man sat inches from us, the man whom we knew had killed Jennifer, spoke of disgusting things he now had no want to conceal. At one point, I found myself unable to listen to further disclosures too repugnant for me to here describe. And through it all, he spoke as though his normality accredited him with acceptance to all who heard. I refused to accept more pain. I think I'm made of stronger stuff, but getting Andrew to excuse me, I tried quickly to leave the court. In the end, we left together. How could we listen to him any longer? The media reported that I was in tears, perhaps I was. Yvonne accompanied us. Did Black take further gratification from this? Perhaps he did. I didn't care. My husband often says that as a grown man of sixty-two years old, he assumed he had heard everything! Nothing came near to what we were hearing and what we were putting ourselves through, spoken by the man sitting before us. Apart from this brief lapse, we braced ourselves to continue. God held us.

When the jury heard the explicit illustrations given by Black when his interrogator, Pamela, asked what place he would think suitable to stop to take a little girl, they asked that they might drive by coach from Jennifer's home to the site of her abduction. The minibus took the twelve men and women along the road she had cycled. This had been his prime mistake and the one that cost him dearly, the time when God "opened the donkey's mouth".

In Black's own words, "a tree-lined road sweeping down a hill and round a gentle bend, with a house set back on one side". The description proved literal and was to become his undoing.

Police with the jury made their way along the route. They had set up the required roadblocks around our house. A friend had called, able to stay only a short while, and I valued his company. It was eerily quiet, our road devoid of traffic, with a heavy air of sobriety. Alone, I watched the minibus slowly pass the house, escorted by police cars before and behind. My silent remembrance was of an August day thirty years earlier, this memory now replaced with cruel reality. Andrew soon arrived, having been held up by the roadblocks.

We also sat through the sad matter of the post-mortem medical findings which were shown on screen. Presentations were given from more than one expert. We suffered the nature of the sexual assaults. It was especially hard for Andrew.

Later someone reported Andrew's response, "For thirty years we as a family really have never tried to understand or to think of what, in the last hours of her life, Jennifer went through, and all of a sudden we were confronted with the awfulness of those last few hours and what she would have had to suffer. That has been truly awful for every one of us."

God is not a high-in-the-sky God but a with-me God who brings His nearness to us. "For I, the LORD your God, will hold your right hand, Saying to you, 'Fear not, I will help you'" (Isaiah 41:13). Yes, days will sadden us, days can crush us, but, this God is above every one of them.

20

DAYS, WHEN WILL THEY EVER END?

Armagh is a city, its name derived from the term "Ard Macha", named after the place where St Patrick built his church on the hill of Macha. It is a small town, with an iron-railed garden across the road from the court. Often we would go there for a walk at lunchtime – great for some fresh air, and great for head clearing, the Armagh weather being kind. We found it good to fix our eyes on something different from court figures, and it was good to remember that the world still revolved around its everyday affairs. Lorry and van drivers still leaned on their horns, hungry young people still enjoyed their burgers, and traffic wardens still kept their pens occupied.

Media, on the other end of microphones and cameras, were continually around but they have our thanks and appreciation for their courteousness to us. We did get to know some quite well, and I now believe few of them to have an easy job.

The conclusion of the trial was in sight. As a family, we had sat together for more than six weeks, each day fearing what we would yet have to hear. Grief for thirty years had been so rooted in our home that I thought we were now made of stronger stuff. If she was still alive, Jennifer would have been thirty-nine. To all of us, she will always be nine years old.

Almost at the end of October, trees showing their colours, we drove along country roads engaged with little of their beauty. The man who held the plea of innocence sat continuously with us like an onlooker. We waited for his charge of guilty. We knew what he had done. The Lord, who lifted us up, held us up. Each day of trial, I took His word in Psalm 109 verse 7 by faith, "let him be found guilty".

It was seventeen years since Robert Black had been on the receiving end of Mr Toby Hedworth. Then a junior counsel, two years later Toby became one of the finest prosecution Queen's Counsels in England, a formidable assailant who knows well his every opponent.

Many years ago, in beautiful Co. Kerry, our caravan holiday with Philip and Victoria, who were then still quite young, would soon be over, the Irish weather blisteringly hot. Before leaving, an ageing fisherman shared some freshly caught crab with us, and hearing Andrew voice his regrets in our holiday being over, he said these words, often reiterated by my husband, "Son, all things good and all things bad come to an end."

It was time for the end. Both sides were to address the jury for the last time. As Mr Hedworth took the lead, he reminded the jurors of the facts: those presented throughout the case, divulged from Bad Character Evidence, and particularly those which ascertained Similar Fact Evidence. Of these were several, among them his manner of abduction and abuse, his stated sexual preference for young girls, his knowledge of country roads, and his ease, within the pursuit of his job, of discarding their bodies in laybys and in water.

One unfounded fact of similar evidence was this: all children since Jennifer were found with their shoes removed. Mr Spens put notable significance on the fact that Jennifer was wearing shoes, while other recovered bodies were not. I would like to have had the opportunity to say in this regard that Jennifer, albeit nine years old, was a very strong little girl, an able tree climber, living with two brothers, constantly playing with other boys. My view is that, in not removing Jennifer's shoes, Black suffered as Jennifer tried to defend herself. Forcibly removing the shoes of his later victims would give his assaults an easier expediency. No bodies before Jennifer were ever retrieved, so I seriously wonder if Black found Jennifer's defence caused painful wounds he was unable to explain.

All these things sound horrific, even macabre, but such was what we had to learn through the trial and hearings of those six weeks. I have no wish to portray anything further that may be considered unwarranted upon the feelings of my readers, but this is the man: this is Robert Black.

Toby Hedworth gave the jury his final words. They were recorded and printed in the media: "Mr Hedworth was never so impressive than during his two-and-a-half hour closing statement culminating in dramatic fashion as he turned to Black in the dock and asked the jury why he had refused to give evidence.

'There is one absolutely central and fundamental witness that I, on behalf of the prosecution, would have liked to have asked some questions. Questions to assist you in your careful and thorough and fair examination of this case. But, strangely this witness is not dead. He is not infirm. He is not unable to come to court.

'He has, in fact, been here in the centre of this court for the duration of the trial. But he has quite deliberately chosen not to walk the few short paces from the dock to the witness box – you can make your own assessment, but I make it eight paces – take the oath, look you in the eye, and answer these charges.

'You may ask yourselves why. Because, ladies and gentlemen, the prosecution would have some questions for Robert Black. Questions that, because he is guilty, he knows he cannot answer'".[4]

---

[4]   "Serial killer Robert Black guilty of another murder." *Evening Chronicle*, 27 October 2011, https://www.chroniclelive.co.uk/news/north-east-news/serial-killer-robert-black-guilty-1406294. Accessed 10 June 2021.

Seldom has Mr Toby Hedworth sounded so grave. As he wrapped up the prosecuting evidence to the jury, he brought them step by step to what should be confident conviction.

Always, and rightly so, the final engagement with jurors from both Queen's Counsels is that of Defence. Knowing his expertise, we were not surprised as Mr Spens, ably assisted by Mr Paddy Taggart, his junior counsel, presented the jury with all speculated disparities in the given Similar Fact Evidence. Evidently, the predominant and well-noted similarities would far outweigh any alleged doubts. Both Counsels had neglected nothing of worthy consideration, laying with precision all presentations to the jury.

On Tuesday morning, 29th October 2011, Judge Weatherup brought his directives to the jury to a close. I had wondered how this man, this seasoned judge, could bring words to focus these men and women, almost shattered from previous procedures, upon their final duty. But this was a man of professionalism, a man of proficiency, and a man of experience, "All right-thinking people would be appalled at what they have heard about this defendant. You would be naturally outraged when hearing this man's previous convictions. You would want to throttle him or worse if he came near to any member of your family. It is understandable, given what you know of him, emotions can run high. But I want you to stop, step back and be objective. I want you to know you must judge the matter on the basis of evidence. The onus is upon the prosecution to prove his guilt, and not on the defendant to prove his innocence. You must also assess what inference you will draw from the accused's decision not to take the stand. You cannot help but feel sympathy for the family, and the victim in this case. Nevertheless you must look at the matter dispassionately and view the evidence."

The jury began their deliberations that Tuesday morning. They left the court singularly, and quietly, no one envying their task. Andrew and I could not believe this dreaded trial was finally coming to an end. Everything was in the hands of the unknown twelve men and women.

Our family room meant much to us, a place to rest, a place to talk, a place to hide. A place from where we could look out on an outside world, a world in which we seemed unable to claim any further part. The first-floor window showed us shops and car park, squabbling children with harassed parents, joggers deftly missing pedestrians; lives that were being lived, while we were spent and emptied.

Each morning Andrew and I still spent time with Christ reflecting on His death and resurrection. We took every promise ratified by His death, and made it our own. This brings a wonderful reality of God. We need to know Him, so that we can trust Him. God calls this fellowship – and it is priceless.

Thursday was the third day of jury deliberations. There were many gathered with us in the room, most expecting to be there for some considerable time. Raymond, Stephen and Andy, with Yvonne as always, were great support. They had put immense work into the trial. Time was stealing away from us. If the jury took much longer perhaps it was because they could not reach agreement. They told us it would take as long as it would take. The jury had left with a large weight of script. It was the first trial taken in Northern Ireland upon Similar Fact Evidence. Would it pay off? I wished I had police experience of courtrooms. I escaped to the nearby ladies' room.

"Lord, I know Your Word. I know Your will of judgement upon this man. Why are they taking so long?"

Alone I looked into the mirror which now looked back at me as I prayed, voicing my doubts, feeling tears fill my eyes. Somehow I realised God was very close. Words I knew so well took hold of me.

"Now this is the confidence that we have in Him, that if we ask anything according to His will, He hears us. And if we know that He hears us, whatever we ask, we know that we have the petitions that we have asked of Him" (1 John 5:14–15).

"When he is judged, let him be found guilty. And let his prayer become sin" (Psalm 109:7).

Just Jesus and me. I loved Him and asked forgiveness for being so doubtful right when it mattered. So I smiled, brushing the tears away. Just two steps across the hallway and I was back in the room where everyone was quiet. But I wanted to shout. I wanted to shout that I knew the jury would be back quickly, back with their unanimous guilty verdict. Why didn't I? I sat down beside our Pastor Jimmy, telling him what had happened, but no one else, Andrew being on the far side of the room. Suddenly there was a call. The court now quickly summoned us to take our places. The bailiff had informed the judge they had reached their verdict. Many feet make a lot of noise.

The court was packed. The jury, their faces I noted were gaunt and grave, yet revealed nothing. They were embracing one another as they came in to take their uncomfortable seats for the last time. As I watched each of them, I loved them. And I loved Jesus. He and I knew the outcome, and our family felt His nearness. Judge Weatherup addressed the room in weighty tones asking for respect and quietness when the verdicts were read out. The clerk of the court arose, and then the forewoman of the jury arose.

"Have you reached your verdict?"

The court heard her solemn answer, "Yes, your Honour, we have."

The rest of my life would hang upon the words that were about to be uttered.

Robert Black sat in the dock, handcuffed between the two police officers, a female guard to his right, a male guard to his left. He betrayed no nerves, nor any false impression of "What have I done?" or "Why did I do it?" His anarchical "who cares" demeanour tried to belittle the awful integrity which the court weighed upon every soul within it. He sat nonchalant in old jeans, worn grey jumper, with hands clasped on his lap. I watched him in front of me. Was he remembering Jennifer? I knew that he was. God remembered her too, and He remembered her family.

"When He avenges blood, He remembers them; He does not forget the cry of the humble" (Psalm 9:12).

The blue slip of paper was passed from the clerk of court to Mr Justice Weatherup. He received the paper, read it with neither spoken statement nor facial expression, and returned it in quietness. The time was 12.04 p.m. No one breathed. No one moved. To the charge of Kidnap, the standing forewoman of the jury gave a clear response.

"Guilty."

To the charge of Murder, the declaration was the same.

"Guilty."

It held a timelessness within it that pervades the court.

The given verdict was unanimous. As a family we sat together, but at that moment unknown to any others, we each felt a sudden aloneness. Jennifer was the only one near to us. She held us with such a sweet presence in all that she meant to us, as our daughter, our sister, yet in another sense neither before nor since have we felt more united, never before with more empathy. The court remained so silent. Tears were overwhelming. Andrew quickly held me as we wept together. I could not lift my head. He held Victoria, and we embraced our two boys. I felt for each of them, after thirty years and eleven weeks. As all eyes of the court were now upon us, their love tangible.

The court I shall never enter again was quiet. None of my family can recollect seeing any face devoid of tears, including the exhausted jury and media. Judge Weatherup addressed Robert Black who was standing for the hearing of the verdict. The killer looked at no one, all eyes were upon him.

"You have been convicted by a jury of murder. There is only one sentence that will be imposed by law. That is the sentence of life imprisonment. Accordingly, I sentence you to life imprisonment. Take him down, please."

For me those words, "Take him down," (I do not remember hearing "please") will be within me forever, three words, so cold, so authoritative, so final. With the eyes of the judge already imprisoning him, we watched Robert Black, in silent view, taken by his guards out of our sight.

21

DAYS AFTER WORDS

Robert Black began his imprisonment for murdering Jennifer; it is right that the government should exact punishment. But, unlike the murdered children, Black was still alive. He could still play his mind games with these former victims. Today I think of Mr Herkes. Was it not for his spell of gardening on 14th July 1990, possibly, and probably, more little children would have suffered a similar fate, throughout the UK, and further afield.

This would not be the last we would see Black. The date given for his official sentencing was to be in six weeks' time, in Belfast Crown Court. Still in court, the judge passed on his sympathies, heartfelt, to Jennifer's family acknowledging that we had had to live with this for thirty years. He then turned to the jury, saying that, due to the disturbing nature of the evidence in the case, arrangements would be made for a counselling service for each of them.

We spent time with our family, and I so appreciated being with my sister and her husband, accompanied by my niece and her husband. This was difficult for them and I admired their courage.

The verdict was never more important than to the main team of the police investigators. They had each given a painstaking diligence to the hounding of this man for justice and the investigation had become one of the longest open cases, more than thirty years, in criminal history in the UK. This country of Northern Ireland, together with the whole of the UK, owe an immense debt to these men. We are proud of them.

Mr Murray and Mr Clarke said, when questioned, that it was a privilege to lead the police team investigating Jennifer's murder for those nine years. When asked if the eventual conviction had become the most satisfying of their careers, I quote Raymond as saying, "No question." Detective Chief Superintendent Murray's final words hold worthy sobriety, "Robert Black is a lost cause to humanity."

Stephen Clarke said, "Absolutely, to take what we had, develop it to what we did, and present it the way we did from a professional point of view, there's no doubt it doesn't get any better. The details of Robert Black's crimes, as we have heard over the last number of weeks, give a greater insight into him then any words I could ever say. A convicted paedophile, he preyed on the most vulnerable, most innocent, and most cherished members of society – our children – devastating families and communities along the way. Today's conviction will ensure he will remain behind bars for a long time."

Our hearts had warmed to Mr Toby Hedworth and Miss Donna McColgan for their professionalism throughout the case. We shall never forget them. Mr Hedworth planned to pursue more crimes committed by Black.

Toby and Donna, the next day, did something personal and so very touching. Before Toby left to travel home, both made the journey to our little Portmore cemetery where they each left a white rose on her grave. I learned that in England seven years ago at the close of the trial in Newcastle upon Tyne, they had done the same for each of the little victims there. For us it was endearing to see, and will be remembered.

On first writing this book, my most poignant question within my own heart was this, "Shall more be laid on similar little graves?" The negative answer upon Black's death reinforces its pain.

The person whom most people were surprised to see us thank was Mr Spens. I met him alone in the foyer as he left the court. Not knowing that my husband and our two sons had already thanked him, I approached him with an embrace, my face tear stained. I could see he was taken aback. Such is the grandeur of our justice system that every British man holds his innocence until proven guilty, even Robert Black. David Spens put his all into the serious defence of one convicted. Right then David Spens had a depth behind his eyes which met and matched my own, and with his soft words of returned thanks, we touched each other.

Our prayer was that Black, in the face of given factual evidence would be proved unanimously guilty. We had the result. Let us never overlook the word that the Lord gave me, almost two years previously, "When He avenges blood, He remembers them; He does not forget the cry of the humble" (Psalm 9:12); "When he is judged, let him be found guilty, and let his prayer become sin" (Psalm 109:7).

"He does not forget the cry of the afflicted."

God did so for Jennifer's sake.

Our little room, this would be the last time we would refuge here. As a family, we wanted to do one more thing while we were together. We were without bitterness in seeing, for almost two years, a man bereft of salvation, yet with his own blame and his own guilt. For any one of us to enter eternity without Christ – is a step we dare not take. It is also a needless one. I challenge any forgiven soul to wish an eternity of hell upon any other. And Robert Black, without a Saviour, will find as we are told in the book of Jude, "the blackness of darkness forever".

Andrew prayed collectively for him, aware that this same Jesus died not for our sins only, but for the sins of the whole world. Jesus cares. As Andrew was to tell the press in a few moments, we have the glorious hope of eternal reunion with our daughter. This in itself deals with bitterness.

The Clerk of Court was a special lady named Grace, who was so attentive, so helpful, during those six weeks.

She spoke to Andrew that afternoon, tears falling freely. Grace had been on court duty for over thirty years. Throughout all the Ulster Troubles, amidst many scenarios of shootings, bombings, torture and death, she said to Andrew that she had never witnessed such emotion within court. This, as she wept with him, was the worst she had witnessed. Regarding the person of the man Robert Black, her heart failed and words failed. One quote that day from the *Irish News* was this, "Tears were unquenched on the press benches overcome by the moment, as well as from journalists hardened through years of covering violence in Northern Ireland".

Teresa Thornhill, whom Black attempted to abduct in Nottingham, related on television at the time of the broadcasted verdict how she has had to live and suffer with the repercussions of what happened to her. Those like Teresa will seldom know any easy path through life.

One article I read recently was from a reporter named Gail Walker. Gail grew up in the early eighties learning to be afraid. I know that there are many more who have also learnt to fear, not only in Ulster and in the south of Ireland, but also across more of Great Britain, and also in Europe where other young girls have been murdered, their bodies never recovered.

Gail writes of the hushed tones of grown-ups in her presence when news reached them of Jennifer Cardy's disappearance, "Robert Black haunted my childhood as he must have done with hundreds of little girls. He was the faceless Bogeyman, and all the more terrifying for that because I'd no idea who to be on the lookout for, just that he could pounce at any time and there would be no escape.

"From the moment I heard that nine-year-old Jennifer Cardy had gone missing, presumed abducted, I was intensely on my guard. Maybe it was because Jennifer was around the same age as me or that suddenly the sort of murder that only happened in faraway England had occurred just a few miles away, but a darkness crept in around the edges of those summer days spent outside playing with friends that never receded."

Gail's article reflects an experience I had recently when I had the privilege to speak with a woman who told me she also was the same age as Jennifer would be now. She was married with a young family, but through her fear of abduction she could never allow them freedom to be outside on their own, even though they were old enough to do so. Her reason being that, although she never knew Jennifer personally, she had always remembered her, and therefore feared for her children's safety.

She was a Christian. I shared the fact that God is great, and that nothing, and no one, is greater than He. Should we allow our fear to take a greater place, a greater hold upon us, than we allow to Him? Are we accrediting evil, and the fear of evil, with more power over us than a worthy Redeemer has? It was good to see this helped her. It has certainly helped me over many years.

The time had now come for us to speak publicly to the press, to all the media, and they arranged that we would meet in the park in front of the courthouse. I had never seen so many cameras and microphones, and we felt nervous as to how our words would be carried. It was question and answer time. One thing in our favour was the fact that we were speaking to those who cared, and these papers, television and radio news broadcasts would bring the good news, if it could be so called, to the whole of the UK.

So much was happening so quickly. I tried to get our family together but there was always someone out of shot.

Eventually Andrew answered, "Robert Black stole the life of our daughter Jennifer, but Robert Black didn't steal the lives of me and my family – we've lived a happy, prosperous life, but we miss Jennifer each and every day. Robert Black will not destroy us. I would have to say that somebody who commits murders like this, I believe their lives should be taken. I believe they should be put to death, that's my belief. I don't say that in a vengeful way, I mean that in a just, a righteous way.

"For the last six weeks we have had to endure and listen to how Robert Black kidnapped, sexually abused and murdered our daughter and our children's sister and it has been absolutely horrendous. We have heard things that in all honesty wasn't even in our imagination, and for thirty years we, as a family have never tried to think or understand what she must have gone through, and all of a sudden we were confronted with the awfulness of those last few hours and what she would have had to suffer. That has been truly awful for each and every one of us."

Andrew spoke brokenly, but I was glad he did.

Many people were with us. Some rain began to fall, enforcing a reality to the words we were saying. I shared Jennifer's infectious joy of life, her happiness and her endearing ability to further so much happiness in the lives of others, and of her nine-year-old thoughtfulness that went far beyond her young years.

Andrew and I never forget Jennifer. She will always be in our hearts, always missed, and always yearned for. Yes, Robert Black has done this awful deed but I join with my lovely husband and say, he will not destroy us. We will never have closure. The daughter we loved is gone. But we have the relief of knowing that the perpetrator of this gruesome and horrible crime has been brought to justice and that does give us a peace, and a relief. I will also say this: murder, death, trial and trauma, are no match for the grace of God.

As time has gone on, I wish I could have added to the reporters how not one of us had ever been low in her presence, but always refreshed and upbeat, and how she would suddenly appear at my hand to help when rheumatoid illness so restricted me. But I think sometimes of what so many shall never know of Jennifer's final day. How I had sharply, though unknowingly, interrupted her that morning when, in her bedroom, she was having her quiet time with Jesus; but she hadn't got cross with me because she never did. How I had sat outside on our patio, Victoria beside me in the pram that same summer's day, reading a book of fiction while Jennifer fought for her life. How I have refused to read fiction ever since. How I thought I heard the familiar noise of her bicycle being rested against the back wall of our house at the expected time she was due home. How disappointed I had been when hearing silence instead of her little sandalled feet skipping up the kitchen floor, even before I knew anything to be amiss.

Andrew closed by telling the media, "So we leave the court so happy that justice has been done and Robert Black will never again be able to harm another wee girl. He will be in jail until he dies."

22

THERE CAME A
DAY TO THINK

We had many interviews during that time and we tried not to refuse any. There are regrets in not agreeing to some, but, as I've said before, we think too much on the run, and wish we had done otherwise on some never-retrieved occasions. Quite exhausted, the sensitivity with which the media treated us was always touching and respectful, particularly encouraging on our firm's Facebook page. I will say here how ultra-green in computer cognisance we showed ourselves to be. Unfortunately I saw none of Facebook. Andrew saw the wonderful public media backing in his office only because of Philip's innate internet savvy. I think I am right in assuming that this trait has become a new sixth sense to all humankind, excluding those unfortunates who are over sixty years old. Someday I hope to eat my words.

Hillsborough Elim Church was amazing to us. This is our own church and we deeply appreciate all for their love and thoughtfulness, with their faithful prayers. During that first week after the trial, knowing we had become bankrupt those few months before, they quickly, though secretly, gathered quite a large sum of money to offer us a holiday. Pastor Jimmy brought the given surprise to us at home and on opening what I thought to be a greetings card, we were speechless, and that will not often be said for Andrew, and certainly not for me. Love can dumb any tongue.

Life, however, can throw it! An unfortunate thing was about to happen. A holiday was almost booked; we would leave at the end of November to holiday in Rome, a place where we had always longed to go, and we looked forward to this, to having time alone together, to try to climb above what we had come through just the week before. Our church was to host a live radio broadcast on the following Sunday morning. It was quickly organised that Andrew and I were to give an interview during the live service. As we told how able God had been to us throughout the ordeal which we had feared, God was honoured, and all were encouraged. We knew it was a privilege to share what we did.

That evening Andrew had a prearranged church meeting to take several miles away, so I left alone to travel to Hillsborough. It had rained during the afternoon, a sub-zero temperature now showed on my dashboard. I was just a few miles from the church. My car skidded. Unable to retrieve command, dark ice was taking the ownership of the four wheels beneath me, brakes refused my bidding. For the first time in my life, I was responsible for a car that didn't care, preferring to do its own thing, its own way, propelling me to the wrong side of the road. With oncoming traffic I would have been killed. The bank on the opposite side was coming to get me, not only laying demand upon my car but upon all that it contained. How merciful was God as I screamed His name. He spared me fatal impact with a brick wall which I narrowly missed.

Before anyone arrived, I thanked God I was safe. I was still alive. On trying to leave the car, I realised that I had severely damaged my left knee, and that my front driver's door was jammed. Help was with me very quickly, and I could see kind friends from church who phoned Andrew and Victoria. I hoped Andrew had not already left. In view of what we had just the week before come through, how, how could I tell them what had now just happened? I also asked someone to relay a message to church. Police closed the road but very soon Pastor Jimmy arrived, followed by Andrew and Victoria.

Quite ingeniously, after some conflab, the Fire Brigade were able to extricate me from my Ford Fiesta, and an ambulance then conveyed me to the A&E department of Royal Victoria Hospital in Belfast. Andrew, Victoria and Jimmy stayed most of the night with me, the surgical ward accommodating me for the next ten days. The surgeon who operated on my kneecap showed his expertise in metal collage.

Unable to use crutches I was pleased that Victoria willingly vacated her downstairs bedroom to enable me the use of a wheelchair. I had done this before, so I was quite proficient after a day or two of steering, knuckles intact from room to room. Rome sadly had to manage without us.

These days did become for me a quiet time of looking back on all that had happened. I thought about Robert Black. Many were asking us, as a family, to explain how we held no bitterness. The stigma and horrifying modus operandi of this man was well known to all, and it was right that people should be appalled. What is not right is the desire for individual revenge, and a Christian granted grace from a holy God and almighty God ought never to exact personal retribution. However, forgiving is not condoning. I think these two different concepts can cause, and have caused, a lot of confusion, misunderstanding and ill-feeling.

God is more forgiving than we are. We may think, because He is God, it is easy for Him to forgive. The fact is, God sees sin in its deepest propensity, therefore it must be harder for Him to forgive, not easier. He sees sin for what it is, from a holy heart that knows the true horror of it. We, as humankind, have long lost our shock of what we call sin and we live too easily with it. Allow me to repeat: forgiving is not condoning. Jesus, alone on the cross, became that sin and suffered the full condemnation of it. Such is what grace is all about. Even angels cannot understand it.

While we are without bitterness, throughout all of these years we have rightly expected God to apportion His own justice upon all that happened to Jennifer. Robert Black was an evil man and few have ever aspired to such evil. We serve a God who is just and we have known and trusted our God enough to avenge such wrongdoing inflicted upon Jennifer, and upon us. God owns a righteous justice, and tells us, "He who says to the wicked, 'You are righteous,' him the people will curse; nations will abhor him. But those who rebuke the wicked will have delight, and a good blessing will come upon them" (Proverbs 24:24–25).

23

SENTENCING

Christmas shoppers were beginning to search out the best places to park that cold wet morning as Andrew drove us to a more foreboding occasion. Our rain-bespattered car carried Andrew and me in the front, Victoria, Andrea our granddaughter, and brother-in-law Brendan in the back, my wheelchair ensconced with a cushion in the boot. A prime car parker, Andrew soon got us a kerbside location close to court. I often say that he can position a car more deftly in a space than a box of matches within its holder.

The date for the sentencing of Robert Black had been arranged for the 8th December 2011 at Belfast Crown Court. So was seen a party of four people running on a footpath to escape the rain, a lady trundled ahead on a jolting wheelchair, with an umbrella pushed out in front of them. We reached the courthouse somewhat bedraggled and were quickly ushered through security gates. Appropriate composure, I do not know how, we soon recovered.

Philip arrived and we were glad to see him and have his company and support. However, it was unfortunate that Mark was unable to be there. Some friends, including Pastor Jimmy, were also with us, and of course, Yvonne with the well-satisfied police team, Raymond, Stephen and Andy. Court 13 was the setting for the sentencing of Robert Black. The heavy doors of the courtroom opened. All of us knew this would not be pleasant, but we did expect his sentencing to bring some gratifying form of closure after what we had recently come through.

Two weeks previously Black had instructed his defence team to issue an appeal. Already aware of the same procedure in England after his sentencing there, we tried not to allow it to worry us. Appeals are important and by implication cannot be undervalued. The good thing is that we again trusted God, who always goes ahead of us, and leaned this new worry upon Him.

The courtroom for the sentencing was smaller, and more tightly packed than the one in which the trial took place. Police, journalists and the media reporters, with our family and friends, were in public seating, and I wondered where Andrew and I, being wheelchair bound, would sit. Ushers placed us to the left side of the room, while Philip and Victoria were seated to our right, directly to the rear of Robert Black, under guard in the dock. I watched as they sat, both so still and stoic. My heart felt for them and admired them.

The press reported that Victoria who sat, for the first time behind Black, was "stony faced behind him, her pale face a ghostly reminder of the young life snuffed out by Black on that fateful trip in August 1981".

And I watched him there: the same zombied Robert Black, without expression, empty-eyed and empty-minded. He wore the same blue jeans, white t-shirt and grey jumper. He seemed to just appear, and I wondered how I never saw him being brought past me. Then I realised he is always brought from under floor chambers straight to the courtroom dock. I hated that we had to see him again.

I felt that I could not view his unforgotten face. But nor was I able to blind my eyes to see those cruel hands that were comfortably holding his cup of water. Was he thinking? If so, what was he thinking? Was he again seeing Jennifer's face? Was there any hint of guilt, any uncovered remorse? I felt sure there was none. Or maybe he was thinking how stupid he had been that day in Stow, twenty-one years ago, when he decided to double back to keep another work appointment.

Judge Weatherup entered as everyone stood dutifully to their feet. I did too. But here was a man now quite formidable, clearly focussed and resolute for all that should be done. As we took our seats he held my confidence. We waited.

Robert Black remained silent. The court directed all things towards him and against him. He was a captive. Somehow he looked like one. I thought it strange to see him again within six weeks. He was older. Toby Hedworth put the charge to the judge that Black should face a whole life term given his other killings. We certainly agreed with that. Mr Spens, unusual for defence counsel, gave no plea for mercy. He offered no mitigation on the behalf of Robert Black to the judge. He said, and I will always remember the clarity with which he said it, "This is one of those rare cases in which there is no mitigation, and so I propose to say nothing in that regard."

Victim Impact Statements were asked of us. Philip gave one as well. How hard I had found this to be. How does anyone write words on paper to convey the effect the murderer of your child has had upon your life for over thirty years? I was unable to do so. I wrote some words but in the end, I found I could agree to none, and felt unable to sign my name to any. Andrew appreciated my feelings, signing the statement for himself.

The judge read these words from the given paper, "Her father speaks poignantly about Jennifer, of the family's awareness of Jennifer's absence from all family occasions, and of the harrowing revelations in the course of the trial. Jennifer's brother was a six-year-old boy who lost his sister. He speaks of fear and dread of a child's nightmare of the family being targeted again, and of dreams of what Jennifer's last words were, and how she would have struggled in her final hour."

Jennifer was loved too much for us to find the right words to speak of what her murder meant to our living. I know how difficult this was to all our family and I gladly attribute high regard that they were able to do that which I could not. I do wish now that I had.

Judge Weatherup continued, and said to Black, "This is such a case where your culpability is exceptionally high and the victim was particularly vulnerable."

He spoke of how Black had always planned to take advantage of any opportunity and by sad mischance Jennifer Cardy became that victim.

"You abducted a nine-year-old girl from near her house. Your crime was particularly serious. You subjected a vulnerable child to unpardonable terror and took away her life. By the manner of that loss, you also have wounded forever a family that treasured that child. It was a wicked deed."

Mr Weatherup sentenced Robert Black to twenty-five years of imprisonment without parole, and four years imprisonment for kidnapping.

Guards handcuffed the killer and led him away. It felt so different from the giving of the verdict that day in Armagh only six weeks before. Court 13 saw no emotion, no relief, and no reaction. All felt that we had nothing left, that we all had been emptied. Somehow, it was good.

The press, unable again to interview us within the court precincts, were respectfully patient while Northern Ireland was doing what it loves – winter wind and rain. Victoria accompanied Philip, having been asked to go to a nearby hotel for a television interview.

We had got to know Gordon Adair, TV news reporter, since the beginning of the trial. Philip and Gordon had grown a mutual rapport. He and Victoria that day answered engagingly well to Gordon, both of them incredibly moving as they shared their life since Jennifer died. Philip remembered when she disappeared and spoke of the trauma he underwent as a six-year-old. He also shared how he grew up without bitterness. What Victoria said was different. She had become the only one in the family without personal remembrances. And at thirty years old, she spoke of being only a baby when Jennifer was murdered. She also spoke, and I loved her for this, of the freedom, in such circumstances, that we had given to each of our children as they grew up, and we admired them both for their touching ability in the answers given to the interviewer's questions. My respect goes to Gordon for his handling and professionalism of that broadcast discussion.

The press again recorded a touching statement, "The sight of Jennifer Cardy's father pushing her mother in a wheelchair into Court 13 in Belfast Crown Court was one of the most poignant images of the day."

We said our goodbyes and met with the press again at the arctic court gates some minutes later. Andrew, as her father, answered the questions put to him regarding his feelings on having seen Black sentenced to twenty-nine years imprisonment.

"It has been an emotional couple of hours. It has been a long, long journey. It has been thirty years of a journey. We are very, very pleased. We think that justice has been done. We don't think Robert Black will be out of jail again to assault little girls. He will never be able to torture little girls."

It certainly gladdened my heart to hear him say that he hoped this family's horrific experiences across the years would help others find the reality of Christ. Through decades of sorrow, he said, this has been our strength. As I listened to Andrew reply, even in such weather, I was proud of him, proud of his portrayal of a living gospel, and proud of the reality he shared of it. This gospel, the Bible calls it glorious, proves itself relevant to every life, and to every dark day within every life.

The media asked my response to the killer's continuing denials of guilt. I had no answer to that, and said that I could only speculate that Black had a great deal to learn regarding this putrid weight of evil. This evil had caused destruction not only in the lives of little victims but to the many families of those victims; clearly upon his own life as well. Had the man known this, he would admit his guilt.

From the interrogation tapes, Black referred to how he always wanted to take little girls, how he always wanted to be with them – I could add more to this. He acknowledged on the tapes how wrong he knew that to be. It did come across that he loathed what people thought of him, and here I saw a man who wished he could turn the clock back. In more sombre terms, he knew and we knew that he would forever be at the mercy of his sordid depravity. But I reckon the man knew that he could enjoy so being. How would I feel were he to ask me to forgive him? We cannot theorise this. It will always be personal, always put to the edge. I answered as honestly as I could when asked about forgiving him: "This family has not suffered from cancerous bitterness. If we had, such bitterness would have robbed us of everything … I've never been asked to forgive Robert Black. Were he to ask me for forgiveness, I would meet him face to face."

That last statement took headline news. To be honest I wished Robert Black would ask to meet me, meet us. I was aware of the pain we would suffer, but then no one can appreciate what it means sharing with any man, however sinful, that which Christ has done for him. God told us this is foolishness to the world, but He uses foolish preaching to save those who believe. I say again, forgiving is not condoning. Forgiveness is neither sensible nor fair. Justice is fair. Forgiveness is the grace of God, and never without cost.

24

AN AWARDING DAY

Something had happened in our home, shortly after Robert Black's conviction that October in Armagh Court. It was one of November's grey days, when I received an unexpected phone call. *Belfast Telegraph*, one of the most widely-read newspapers in Northern Ireland, with whom we had already given interviews, were phoning me with a surprise invitation. When I answered the phone, I expected it to be another request for Andrew and I to talk with a journalist, but, on hearing what this entailed, I was taken aback.

The Northern Ireland Woman of the Year awards would take place in a few weeks' time, and the caller was inviting me to attend the presentation. The *Belfast Telegraph* had received nominations with my name given for the award of Inspirational Woman of the Year. The lady on the end of the phone waited politely for my response.

Flustering and blustering always came easily to me nor did it desert me on this occasion. The fact that I have no recollection of anything I said clearly implies its evidence. Our postman delivered her formal letter to me a few days later.

We knew that the date for the ceremony was the same date given for the court sentencing of Robert Black, at Belfast Crown Court. This gave us a reluctance to attend, but I chose not to share this with the *Belfast Telegraph*. With the thought of another appearance of Robert Black, and what that would entail, we had enough on our plate.

One of Belfast's most prestigious hotels was the setting. It was a black-tie affair. I do wish I were one of those ladies who relish such extravaganza. Unfortunately, I am not! Two lovely things did stand in my favour, though: Susan, our daughter-in-law, is a professional hair stylist, ably taking me under her wing to do my hair and make-up, and a friend at church who took the time to organise needful fittings, is the manager of a well-customised dress shop in Lisburn. Specialist helpers – how I valued them. I chose a beautiful bodice-beaded black dress, the wheelchair forbidden to present problems. Women are good at that.

The morning arrived. We had all lunched, after the sentencing of Black, at the loving expense of a friend in a relatively new restaurant very close to the court. After such a morning, we were feeling grim but we learned to relax with friends and family. There was something that felt very strange as we arrived home that afternoon.

On stepping out of the car, for me and I think for us all, nothing seemed normal. I thought of Jennifer, and how much I still missed her after those long ongoing years, almost expecting to see her appear, as though she had never left us. Right now our house seemed to know an emptiness too. Usually we could pick up the reins, but I kept such thoughts to myself.

That's when it hit me. We would go tonight, and we would enjoy tonight. Maybe our amazing God, always six jumps ahead, had programmed this surprising evening for us. These two events, one so sombre, the other quite up-beat, were incongruous, as if they were something to which no one could relate to at any one given time. Andrew and I decided to go – with no excuses. All hands on deck!

I was in the car and we soon arrived at the hotel. The given programme included a fashion parade. The last one of these I had attended had been Susan's, held in Lisburn for her salon promotional, and was well enjoyed, and very well presented. Afterwards a grand dinner was also scheduled and was beginning to whet everyone's appetite. My escort was a tall handsome man, fitly attired in dress suit with all the trimmings. Mind you, he was accompanying a glamorous lady!

A wheelchair is a brilliant thing and, like any good innovation, it impresses with its simplicity. This was my fifth time viewing the world from a lower horizon. For someone unable to walk it does afford needed mobility and independence, yet for every life we see before us in the person installed in such conveyance, there are drawbacks. One thing which I have been aware of, though certainly not always, is that being alone in a wheelchair among a group of vertical conversationalists can bring an experience of being somewhat, though never intentionally, unnoticed.

The problem is that to a person in a wheelchair, chat is slightly out of range, as they remain below their company's eye level. Conversation therefore can become easier to continue amongst those who are standing in closer eye proximity. I do admit how harsh this sounds, and detract any blame I falsely label. I think, however, it may be a good thing to discern.

Maybe it is a subject we ought to engage with, for before I had been in this driver's seat I was unaware of any such impression being valid. Because we are so often outside that to which others are sensitive, we remain ill-equipped in ascertaining the simple things that affect their lives. For instance, can you think of the last time in a shop where you thought to reach something down to the level of the frustrated wheelchair shopper? When did any designer think to install bar shelves at wheelchair level? I know I found them to be out of reach when Andrew was not at my side.

But I loved where I was and I loved meeting so many people that night, many of whom have left, to this day, a great impression with us both. We talked with those who had given a selfless lifetime to charity work. It was a revelation, showing disciplined hard work, all too often unappreciated. I had come to this event simply to enjoy the happening, and it was evident that these people whom I was meeting deserved their every given award.

As hotels go, this one was quite opulent. The dark, wet, car park belied the white and cream marble fittings that welcomed us. While for the second time that day we battled with Ulster weather, some dutiful tray-bearing waiters ushered us to a fairy tale setting of pinks and whites where cameras were flashing to capture what might soon be forgotten memories. Couples were milling about, several in groups. Andrew and Pat were beginning to feel a little bit out of water! My husband, however, is a good chair pusher, and better still, he is a good stop-and-chat pusher, a very accommodating Andrew trait. This man knows quite a lot of people. Andrew Cardy – he always was my Knight Gallant!

Everyone was finding their seats (I had brought my own, of course!) in the lavish dining hall. It was nice to find ourselves in the company of an interesting group and we made our introductions. Each of the nominees invited to attend were asked to bring a companion, one lady had brought her daughter. She was a delight to be with, totally engaging, and for her young years, she impressed us all with a witty repartee to Andrew who kept her in fun.

The evening had plenty to delight, the fashion parade bringing the outspoken "mms" and "aahs". It should be said that as I looked around, later watching the winners walk to accept their awards, the audience were awarded even more displays of bejewelled dresses. The evening was proving a happy occasion, a brass band having introduced us to dinner. Wendy Austin, the TV presenter, is popular with everyone in Ulster and after she introduced us to a noted magician who mesmerised us with his stuff, the Belfast "Oscars" ceremony duly commenced.

What I had not envisioned was the fact that Belfast had become a Los Angeles spinoff. Each category, of which there were ten, gave four nominees, showing on a large screen the reasons for their choosing. Warm applause conveyed the depth of appreciation for each proposal – Education, Voluntary, Sportswoman, Health, Mother, Inspirational, Business Woman, Fashion and Arts. The night would be finalised with the overall Woman of the Year Award, a worthy title.

"And the winner for the award of Inspirational Woman of the Year is ... Mrs Patricia Cardy."

They had just shown news footage of Jennifer's disappearance followed by pictures of Robert Black, the convicted culprit, with myself and Andrew attending the trial engagements. Those with us at our table gave us smiles of encouragement, though unable to keep from quickly wiping escaping tears and as they ushered us to begin the walk to the platform; we loved them for it. Andrew began to wheel me away from the table, while all I could think of was that I deserved no award. The wheelchair began its journey. Something then happened which neither of us expected, nor shall we ever forget. The whole of the room rose to their feet to give us a standing ovation. The applause intensified as Andrew pushed me onwards and upwards to the presentation area, along the zigzag route for the wheelchair. After the earlier trauma of the day, which the evening news had shown, we were both wiping tears. The audience applause continued until we were again seated.

The very lovely award given to me was an engraved Belleek vase, also a gift of beautiful Belleek jewellery. Belleek is renowned in Northern Ireland, and indeed throughout the UK, as fine Irish Pottery, famous in its own right, and it is a privilege to display this beautiful vase in our home. Each time I look at it, I still feel the same uplift, still feel that heart-warming encouragement, and I am still aware of the same undeservedness. We both are. Yes, I continue to hear the applause, and I see the tears on many faces. Sometimes I still feel my heart shake. Ulster people are exceptional.

The climax of the evening was the presenting of the Woman of the Year Award to Mrs Nuala Kerr who had also received Mother of the Year award. Terrorists had killed her son, Ronan, at the age of twenty-five, earlier that year with a booby trap bomb under his car. This was especially hard for Nuala after the loss of her husband.

Ronan was killed for no other reason than he was a young Catholic police recruit who had joined the PSNI – Police Service of Northern Ireland.

Nuala's words through the media the day following her son's death became the stabilising of what could have been further violent reaction in Ulster during a tentative peace process. She bravely encouraged all Northern

Ireland's Catholic recruits. This callous act, she said then, should not allow Ronan to die in vain.

Nuala said these words, "We all need to stand up and be counted, and strive for equality. We don't want to go back to the dark days of fear and terror. We were so proud of Ronan and all that he stood for. It's a sad day for our community." Nuala accepted the award to another deserved standing ovation, and simply said, "I'm very honoured – for Ronan's sake. I never expected to win this."

It was a time to remember as I embraced Nuala at the end of the evening and spoke to her and her lovely family. We had so much in common in the tragic and yet so different loss we both shared. A heartfelt empathy was forged between us, and I think back with remorse of not having tried to keep in touch with her. Why do we allow time to pass us by, and rob us of the little things that we could have done? The evening was good. God had surprised us again. And we were glad. So ended a night of celebration, where women acquired honour for their commitment at every level, many at personal cost. All showed effort, gut-determination, and a never-say-die resilience. Each of us can learn from that!

25

"WHY" DAYS THAT BRING NO ANSWERS

It was said to Andrew by one of his customers, "You know Andy, if there were no luck but bad luck, you would be the luckiest person I know."

Thinking that quite witty, we could both see the logic behind it. It does raise questions, one of which is, "Where is God in all of this?" Or, better still, "*How* could God be in all of this?"

It is expected that if God is on our side, nothing should cause us grief. I support the truth that God is able to deliver His people from all attacks of evil. Life has shown itself tough, maybe ours a lot more so than others, but His presence in our lives has been a powerful reality within every dark day and every dark situation where Satan seldom pulls his punches.

When I was only eight years old, after my mother had died from asthma, I found something out: I never did mind being on my own, always finding something new to do. Life was good with fields to walk through, and the best thing was that there were trees to climb (in retrospect, Jennifer also had this talent). I recall the day I climbed a stone pillar beside the road which guarded the gated entrance to a field. I should say that when only eight, all pillars are big. I climbed expertly to the top peak, where I positioned myself uncomfortably to view unfamiliar cars. Well, life was innocent then. But life being very innocent, I had more serious things to put my mind to.

Imagination played an important part in our school playground games. It was a Saturday and I had to think of new ideas to reach the moon before Monday. Would it be on a golden shooting star? Better, perhaps we could have a shining golden coach driven by eagles! Well, I did say life was innocent. "Moon, stars, gold, jewels, coaches etc." All so glamorous, but I knew, wistfully, these would never be mine. As I watched black cars pass under my eye-line at their scary thirty miles-per-hour, I became conscious of a different thought, and, at such a young age, I was aware that this thought was not my own. Like a newsflash holding our screens, the following thought implanted itself, "If I am happy, I will never need them." Suddenly I knew a truth which many have never uncovered. Happiness cannot be reliant upon things which we have or do not have. I was eight years old.

2003 and university life was over. Victoria and her friend Rachel had decided to indulge on a gap-year. She was twenty-two years old, having finished her degree and teacher qualifications, her first at De Montfort University, the second at Bath Spa University, both in England. The girls had travelled in South Africa and then on to Australia, staying with Andrew's cousin, Simon, and his family in Brisbane. It was good to receive phone calls from her, especially that first Christmas she was away. They were enjoying the sun and eating salads, unheard of tropical fish cooked on barbeques and luscious fruit. We were having a glowing home fire, delicious turkey roasting in the oven, with Granny's homemade Christmas pudding. But Christmas was gone and New Year had arrived. The Great Barrier Reef was calling the two explorers.

It was Tuesday morning, 6th January 2004 when the phone call came. My friend Vi would be waiting for me at our first Art Class of the New Year. Why, I kept asking myself, was I refusing to go? I stood fastened to my kitchen floor, hearing the phone ringing. Why was I refusing to answer my phone? It was ringing again. This time the ring was peremptory. I had to answer.

The night before, I had sat on the side of our bed and prayed for Victoria. Australia is a big place. The time difference always eluded me – had she left for the Barrier Reef yet? I focussed upon simple words I felt constrained to pray, "Lord, I pray you will keep Victoria safe on those Australian roads."

The phone was in my hand, the noise stopped.

"Mum, it's me ... I'm in hospital ... I've broken my neck!"

As I write, the recollection of those moments are quietly battling to refill my eyes with tears that I thought should be long gone. The voice sounded like Victoria's, but that was all I could familiarise myself with. She had said something that could not be true. For those few seconds my senses made no sense. She was telling me now that she would be all right, and as she spoke she heard my tears, and I remember her quiet voice anxiously coming through to me in Ballinderry, thousands of miles away, "Mum, I'm going to be all right. Don't cry."

Some familiar strength was holding me, a peace that went beyond my littleness. I told her, as I tried quickly to grasp words I knew to be true, that the Lord would bring her through this, that she must trust Him. We would be with her soon. Words and thoughts even by phone so far apart, were voicing a beautiful reality between us. I was glad to hear her voice.

I knew why I had refused to leave the house. And when I had heard the phone ring, I knew why I had been unable to answer it. God often prepares us to receive harsh news. I have known this many times. My Father had me in a quiet place with Him. We have all had days we will never forget. This day had taken the early ground of comfortable ordinariness. But my eyes were now set upon some different horizon, if one was in sight at all. Sometimes we find the world in which we comfortably live dares to spin on different axes. Nothing is where we left it.

Earlier Victoria had phoned Andrew at work when I had not answered. Philip took the call, and met Andrew in their car park when he returned. Andrew shall always remember, when arriving home, his own deadening feeling of weakness. It was too much, the pain being more than he could bear. Victoria was half a world away. He went for a run. As I awaited his return, and prayed, I saw him return with a new strength. Plans for Australia were implemented. God is "a very present help in trouble" (Psalm 46:1). No day in any life has ever been a problem to Him, and none of our days shall ever be His first. It was good to see we could prove this.

We left two days later, flying from Belfast to Australia, an arduous journey, but on arrival we met with Simon. Simon worked for Brunei Airlines and was a great help to us both. We reached Rockhampton Airport, hiring a car to take us to the hospital. We were told how they had first envisaged flying her down to Brisbane, but instead chosen to care for her here in Rockhampton.

On the hot roads of Queensland in the middle of their summer, the van conveying the friends blew a tyre, overturning into a field. While the others were safe, Victoria who had been in the rear of the vehicle, knew as she lay on the dry, sun-drenched ground that something was alarmingly wrong. One of the first things that people who had stopped beside them had tried to do was to put her on her side into the recovery position. Again, by the rich grace of God, she was quick to say no, refusing to let them move her, aware of a strong sensation coursing down her arm. Paramedics were quick to arrive and offered her appropriate treatment. She was to lie on her back, without movement, for three months.

It had not taken our taxi long to reach the hospital, and we found our way to the floor where she had been given a room to herself. They warmly welcomed us. About to take us to see her, an alert was passed from the medical staff for us to come no further, her room quickly filled with nurses, doctors and noise. Andrew and I found ourselves in an ugly unreality. Victoria had just taken medication. Not being able to raise her head when she felt herself about to choke, the alarm was raised. Happily she recovered when rolled quickly onto her side.

We were each suffering a suffocating tightness of our own, and were now tentative as we entered her room. The large horizontal mirror positioned above her slender frame alarmed me, more especially when I saw she could not turn her head towards us as the nurse told her we had arrived. How amazing it was to finally be with her. She was just the same, still smiling, still anxious for us not to worry, and still alive.

Yasna, Andrew's cousin's wife, worked for an estate agent in Brisbane, 400 miles south, and had booked a room for us at a nearby motel. While Andrew could stay only two weeks, I would stay for the three months until Victoria could be given the all clear to travel home. An English couple whom we got to know well, owned and managed the busy motel, and the room provided for us overlooked the river where delightful pelicans daily entertained us. We had asked, on arrival, to board not only ourselves but Victoria's friends. They had known each other a long time and wanted to be with her for however long this may take. As time went on I came to rely much upon them. They were terrific company when I needed it most. Rachel's younger sister had arranged to meet up with the two girls some time later.

Australia is beautiful. It is also hot. For me, this latter feature of the Antipodes affords me little comfort. This was their summer and we were in the high humidity of the Tropic of Capricorn. My husband loves heat, any kind of heat, any temperature of heat. I am more relaxed with a proper Irish climate. Australian nights were something else! With such heat, between forty and fifty degrees centigrade, with heavy humidity, we had the nightly spectacle of astounding rolling thunder and lightning storms. I loved the way such storms proudly competed in skies above us against any formally-staged firework exhibitions.

Rockhampton Hospital proved itself highly commendable. We drove each morning to Victoria. The staff were brilliant with her. She had been fitted with a skull brace which she had last seen fitted on me, some eight years before, when I had undergone surgery for neck fusion. But I had the horrible thing fitted in good old Ulster. Here in Australia the nurses had to keep this metal fitment clear and ultra-hygienic in high temperature humid weather, no mean feat. The cleansing therapy, because the brace had been drilled through skull bone, was both gruesome and painful. She hated it. However no leniency would be tolerated, and the staff taught me the same sordid procedure.

Although it was hard seeing Victoria those mornings, it was encouraging to know how strangely settled she was becoming. Or was this a brave face we were being shown? Each evening her three friends, Rachel, Steve and Ross came with us and on every such occasion laughter, as only the Irish can do, was filling the ward, often with many of the nursing staff, male and female. We shall never forget what followed. Victoria was the instigator of the bizarre plan, though ably abetted by enthusiastic cronies. Rockhampton Hospital may never see this again, though I believe they did recover.

We arrived at our normal time the next morning, wondering at the many smiles now greeting us. Staff were always cheerful, and we innocently returned these smiles. Then we saw it: an X-ray picture shown at the nurses' station. This X-ray portrayed a neck, spine and rib cage, its centre-piece displaying a large metal fork strategically wedged as though accidentally swallowed. Stephen Spielberg would have been impressed.

The previous evening she had broached the idea of hiding something beneath her gown when they would take her in the morning for another X-ray. A fork was the unanimous decision. She even said how she would hold it firmly and discreetly, while being pushed with all her trolley paraphernalia. Well we did laugh at the idea, naively thinking the girl would never have the nerve. Radiologists, in all their professionalism, unwittingly took the X-ray, while Victoria lay in all innocence, the fork well positioned. It took a starring role for all the time she was there, and was given to her to take home as a memento. We still have it.

But Andrew had to leave. Like Victoria, I too put on a brave face as I drove him to the nearby airport. We thought it best to have a quick good-bye, but I watched until he was out of sight, driving alone for the first time back to town. Already missing him, I forced escaping tears to remain intact.

She and I were not to arrive home for another ten weeks. It was, to a certain extent, good to be independent, not having to rely on other drivers, or taxis. The younger company around me kept me on an even keel. I was able to drive them to the beach and if I didn't stay, I would call back in the evening after being with Victoria, and bring them home.

I soon wished I had answers. Mums should have answers. But, with Andrew away, I was being asked the questions which have no answers. I found such questions unfair, not to myself, but to Victoria who lay on her bed rigidly, each day on her back while others were enjoying sunshine, mobility, diversions and plans. In short: enjoying life. For Victoria and Rachel, the next stop would be Fiji, or should have been. Yes, Mums ought to have answers: I was getting the "whys" and they came with tears. That's the thing about Mums, they learn over the years to take it on the chin. In a way, we count it a privilege to have it so. I did give answers, but I did not know the right answers. Are there any right answers? We talked of God, Victoria being a Christian since she was five, now twenty-three. I prayed with her, and spoke to her the truths of God and the truths of His Word – that was good for me too.

The day came. Victoria walked again, very cautiously, but one step at a time she did it! On writing these words my heart is aware of those who have never walked again. What can I say concerning families who hurt? Being bereft of words I hope is understandable.

Teresa Thornhill, the fifteen-year-old English girl, tortured herself with needless guilt because she was alive when others, younger than her, had been not only molested but murdered by the same Robert Black. Whether we like it or not, whether we understand it or not, or have answers or not, such things are not in our hands to control.

I brought Victoria home from Australia with a temporary brace in which she could travel. Our flights were first class, gratefully paid through insurance. I was exhausted, but glad she had the go-ahead to come home some weeks earlier than expected. We said our good-byes to all who had befriended us in Australia. Rachel, her sister Ruth and the boys had left some days earlier having stayed until they saw her walk again. Rockhampton Cathedral of Praise, the church I attended, were more than good to us, taking time to visit Victoria. I was sorry to leave them. We saw a deep sorrow from all who had attended her in hospital, so personally and so lovingly. She had built up a great rapport with all. A sad thing was to happen to Rockhampton. It was devastated by horrendous floods some years later, and we daily viewed on our television screens this town known as the Beef Capital of Australia, which we had come to know so well.

Happily, Victoria recovered well, and a year later, after applying to New Tribes Missions, and finishing her first year of teaching, she was accepted for two years' service in Papua New Guinea to teach in their school, where she was asked to set up an art course, the first one missionary children had been given. This was to be for all ages. She had applied thoughtfully, knowing that God had spared her life, and secured her mobility.

But, like Australia, Papua New Guinea, had more shivers down its spine. It would not be long until this young girl again felt pain. Having witnessed my struggle all her life with the pain and disability of Rheumatoid Arthritis, she was to contract this cruel disease herself. Sent over to Darwin in North Australia for specialist investigation, she was diagnosed with Dengue Fever. This, in itself, was a grave diagnosis, but did give her an overriding relief. On her return to Papua New Guinea the sad news came a week later that the given diagnosis was incorrect. She had the disease that she feared. Victoria now struggled at the mercy of another physical tsunami. I know it was exceptionally hard for her to bear, and longed to be with her.

The questions I put at the beginning of this chapter are deserving of answers. "Where is the reality of God in all of this?" and "How could God be in all these things?"

I can give no other answer to such questions than God in heaven is good to those whom He loves. He cannot be otherwise. We shall often be recipients of evil determination, but the one thing we do know is this – the One who lives in and with every ransomed soul is greater than all the evil that can be thrown against them. Our times are not in the hands of any evil being, but in the greater hands of the One who is in control of all our days. Can we control every circumstance? Perhaps not. However we are in control of all our responses to them.

I have lived my life upon the words God gave me the night I trusted Him so long ago, "Behold, I stand at the door and knock. If anyone hears My voice and opens the door, I will come in to him and dine with him, and he with Me" (Revelation 3:20).

More dark days were soon to come. But for almost fifty years, He has been the rock beneath my feet and the steel within my heart. Holding me with His own incomparable joy, just as He told me at eight years of age when I sat traffic watching.

26

DARK DAYS

Dark days again came upon our family, more hard, difficult days. We were at court again, as was Robert Black. This time before a tribunal of judges assessing his appeal against the guilty verdict of Jennifer's murder. He had instructed his defence lawyers and barristers to have this set in motion two weeks before being given his final sentencing in 2011, and it had taken more than a year to bring it before the court.

Black had lodged appeals before on his convictions of the three murder counts in Newcastle. We were told to expect this. These former appeals had resulted in dismissals, but had caused more grief to the victims' beleaguered families.

Appeals must have serious grounds to dispute conviction, and Robert Black did have a few, presented with the professional expertise from Mr David Spens.

The primary objection was upon the given allowance and admission of Bad Character Evidence presented to the jury. Legalised in 2004 for court presentation, the proviso of it must fall within certain stipulations.

January 2013 brought the face of this man to our unwanted attention again. We may have known little about trials, but we knew even less about appeals, except that we were quick to learn they were assessed purely upon legal requirements. No more witnesses would be called, no more evidence arrayed, no jury installed. Only judges could uphold or dismiss an appeal on these legal grounds, hence the fact that we failed to understand the so-called submissions and their worthy rebuttals which were formally laid before three statesmen-like judges. One thing it did do. It made me acknowledge the immense expertise which our barristers must have; and the worth of their high salaries!

For the fourth time, including the earlier hearings, we were at Belfast Crown Court, this time in the Court of Appeal. Familiar faces were good to see, inspiring the confidence we needed: Raymond, Stephen, Andy and Yvonne, as well as Toby Hedworth and Donna McColgan. Andrew treated us to our morning coffee fix, well-appreciated. The time again being changed for the beginning of proceedings, I began to look around with a more leisurely eye. Not many could afford themselves such respite. I did observe and empathise with tight-lipped families of young men who were making last-ditched attempts against convictions; their angst was hurtful to witness. Many of them recognised us, they were kind to offer their support, which we also conveyed to them. Would they win their own cases? Was this a last-ditched attempt? Perhaps it may be a sad case of, "I fought the law, and the law won."

We were not, however, in these precincts to squander time. Doors were opened with a silence of entry. Minutes later the three robed judges took their places with due solemnity. I found this quite imposing, and saw the authority of the law enforced itself upon all its attendees. The appeal took three days to complete, and we were told the judges would take time to oversee all that was presented to them, and give their ruling at a later date. It was to be another six months before we were called back to court.

Late June, and the judge's verdict was due. I watched the face of Robert Black, our family finding more patience for another unknown decision. Now in the court room we sat together watching the doors open as the three judges entered. Although much of the wider family were not present, once again we felt the holding unity of our togetherness, and once again we felt our aloneness, each with our own thoughts and memories. Robert Black took his seat, again before us.

Judge Morgan wasted no time. Pages of the setting of appeal with their findings upon each were read to the court, without discussions, without questions. The judge was inscrutable. Until he came to these words, "For the reasons given we do not consider that any of the grounds of appeal have been made out. We do not consider that the conviction is unsafe. The appeal is dismissed."

With due ceremony, the three judges took their leave of the court.

It was done, over, finished.

Dad, Mum, Mark, Philip and Victoria embraced each other and the police team for the last time. It was 2013. Our lives forever without Jennifer. Her murderer was led out, his handcuffs familiar, yet veiling nothing of the weight which would tether those hands for the remainder of his life. This man had not only murdered a wonderful daughter, he had murdered the family she loved. I felt sick and quickly looked in the opposite direction, any direction, until for the last time, Robert Black passed me and was gone.

Andrew's words were different. He eyed him as he passed for the last time. "Pat, I watched him as he walked past me. Right then I didn't see Robert Black walk by, I saw hell, and I felt hell, as it passed me."

I will never forget what he said. But with a much more discerning sense, Andrew would remember what had just been impressed upon him.

The body of Jennifer was discovered, returned to her beloved family, and given a proper, worthy internment. There are yet at least ten, perhaps twelve, undiscovered bodies of little girls across the UK, Ireland and continental Europe, which bear the hallmarks of Robert Black. None shall carry, due to his death a year ago, the finality each saddened family has longed to see.

Genette Tate was thirteen years old when she was abducted in 1978 from her bicycle in Aylesbeare, Devon. No trace of the girl who was delivering newspapers has ever been found, and the sight of an overturned bicycle with papers strewn across a country lane will never be forgotten by shocked and saddened viewers. There are striking similarities in the two disappearances of Genette and Jennifer.

Mary Boyle, a little seven-year-old-girl, in Co. Donegal vanished on a spring day in 1977, a year before Genette. She went missing a year after Black got his delivery job in London. Mary was in a rural area with her uncle going across fields when she turned to go back home. She never arrived. Mary was never seen again.

This was to be my plea, my personal and heartfelt plea to Robert Black. How I wish I had got the chance to do so. "Come clean Robert, you have done little that has been good with your life. Do this one thing, tell where they are. It is too late to bring them back. But you can do this one good thing. You will never be too late in doing this." But within three years of the appeal Robert Black was dead.

27

THERE CAME A DAY – THERE WILL COME ANOTHER DAY

God loves today. He gave it to belong to us. Yesterday was today, but will never be again. Neither will tomorrow ever be today. But today is where God is, it is where I am, it is where you are. What can we do now yesterday? What can we do now tomorrow?

But, no more conundrums. Before I knew this amazing God for myself, I nurtured what I called a holy envy – not only wanting but needing what I knew others had. This holy envy pressed me to find Him for myself. Seeing in others a reality of God which I knew I did not have in my own life became a turning point for me. Have I brought you to see a reality of God in my life? In any person's life this should always bring an envy, a holy envy; and rightly so. No one can fabricate the reality of God.

You can close the book, or I think better you can come with me and address whatever your today is. Today will not ruin you, because you know of One who is above every day that seeks to shatter you, and there are days that may just do that. We are, however, at the mercy of none of them. I cannot let you go without reminding you of words that can be your turning point today, as they were to me almost fifty years ago.

"Behold, I stand at the door and knock. If anyone hears My voice and opens the door, I will come in to him and dine with him, and he with Me" (Revelation 3:20).

Who is speaking these words to you? Who is this One standing before you? This is the Someone who loves you, who has already taken your place, and has done everything that needs to be done for you. All that you cannot possibly do for yourself to own the security of heaven and the power of a committed God, is being offered to you. And it is now. Today!

His name is Jesus, and the door at which He stands is the entrance to your heart, to your life. He knocks because of His Lordship to do so. He is the Son of God. Find Him out. When you engage with Him, do not be surprised to learn who He is, and what He has done upon an old rugged cross. Then take Him at His Word.

The Christ who promised to be with me and to bring me through thick and through thin, has been more than faithful in all that He has promised. I know you will agree.

He has done for me more than I can ever convey, and still loves to surprise me. He will do so much more for you.

Maybe you think your life has already been shipwrecked, already ruined. But tomorrow has not yet arrived, has it? You can welcome a new day today, with the God who gives you the reality of a crucified Lord and Saviour, and a great Salvation.

"For God did not send His Son into the world to condemn the world, but that the world through Him might be saved" (John 3:17).

Yes, there comes a day – and it is always today.

Today is the day of salvation. No other day.

You are taking no step in the dark. Faith is acting in obedience, as if the Word of God is true. You are stepping on to the integrity of the Word and the Truth of the God who loves you.

 Publishing

10Publishing is committed to publishing
quality Christian resources that are biblical,
accessible and point people to Jesus.

www.10ofthose.com is our online
retail partner selling thousands of
quality books at discounted prices.

For information contact: **info@10ofthose.com**
or check out our website: **www.10ofthose.com**